Environmental Regulations
and Global Warming

POINT
COUNTERPOINT

Environmental Regulations and Global Warming

Paul Ruschmann, J.D.

SERIES CONSULTING EDITOR
Alan Marzilli, M.A., J.D.

CHELSEA HOUSE
PUBLISHERS
An imprint of Infobase Publishing

Environmental Regulations and Global Warming

Chelsea House
An imprint of Infobase Publishing
132 West 31st Street
New York NY 10001

Library of Congress Cataloging-in-Publication Data

Ruschmann, Paul.
  Environmental regulations and global warming / Paul Ruschmann.
      p. cm. — (Point/counterpoint)
  Includes bibliographical references and index.
  ISBN 978-1-60413-332-5 (hardcover)
  1. Global warming—Law and legislation—United States. 2. Global warming—Government policy. I. Title. II. Series.
  KF3775.Z9R87 2009
  344.7304'6342—dc22   2008035048

Chelsea House books are available at special discounts when purchased in bulk quantities for businesses, associations, institutions, or sales promotions. Please call our Special Sales Department in New York at (212) 967-8800 or (800) 322-8755.

You can find Chelsea House on the World Wide Web at
http://www.chelseahouse.com

Series design by Keith Trego
Cover design by Keith Trego and Alicia Post

Printed in the United States of America

Bang NMSG 10 9 8 7 6 5 4 3 2 1

This book is printed on acid-free paper.

All links and Web addresses were checked and verified to be correct at the time of publication. Because of the dynamic nature of the Web, some addresses and links may have changed since publication and may no longer be valid.

Alan Marzilli, M.A., J.D.
Birmingham, Alabama

The POINT/COUNTERPOINT series offers the reader a greater under-standing of some of the most controversial issues in contemporary American society—issues such as capital punishment, immigration, gay rights, and gun control. We have looked for the most contem-porary issues and have included topics—such as the controversies surrounding "blogging"—that we could not have imagined when the series began.

In each volume, the author has selected an issue of particular importance and set out some of the key arguments on both sides of the issue. Why study both sides of the debate? Maybe you have yet to make up your mind on an issue, and the arguments presented in the book will help you to form an opinion. More likely, however, you will already have an opinion on many of the issues covered by the series. There is always the chance that you will change your opinion after reading the arguments for the other side. But even if you are firmly committed to an issue—for example, school prayer or animal rights—reading both sides of the argument will help you to become a more effective advo-cate for your cause. By gaining an understanding of opposing argu-ments, you can develop answers to those arguments.

Perhaps more importantly, listening to the other side sometimes helps you see your opponent's arguments in a more human way. For example, Sister Helen Prejean, one of the nation's most visible oppo-nents of capital punishment, has been deeply affected by her interac-tions with the families of murder victims. By seeing the families' grief and pain, she understands much better why people support the death penalty, and she is able to carry out her advocacy with a greater sensi-tivity to the needs and beliefs of death penalty supporters.

The books in the series include numerous features that help the reader to gain a greater understanding of the issues. Real-life examples illustrate the human side of the issues. Each chapter also includes excerpts from relevant laws, court cases, and other material, which provide a better foundation for understanding the arguments. The volumes contain citations to relevant sources of law and information, and an appendix guides the reader through the basics of legal research, both on the Internet and in the library. Today, through free Web sites, it is easy to access legal documents, and these books might give you ideas for your own research.

Studying the issues covered by the POINT-COUNTERPOINT series is more than an academic activity. The issues described in the book affect all of us as citizens. They are the issues that today's leaders debate and tomorrow's leaders will decide. While all of the issues covered in the POINT-COUNTERPOINT series are controversial today, and will remain so for the foreseeable future, it is entirely possible that the reader might one day play a central role in resolving the debate. Today it might seem that some debates—such as capital punishment and abortion—will never be resolved.

However, our nation's history is full of debates that seemed as though they never would be resolved, and many of the issues are now well settled—at least on the surface. In the nineteenth century, abolitionists met with widespread resistance to their efforts to end slavery. Ultimately, the controversy threatened the union, leading to the Civil War between the northern and southern states. Today, while a public debate over the merits of slavery would be unthinkable, racism persists in many aspects of society.

Similarly, today nobody questions women's right to vote. Yet at the beginning of the twentieth century, suffragists fought public battles for women's voting rights, and it was not until the passage of the Nineteenth Amendment in 1920 that the legal right of women to vote was established nationwide.

What makes an issue controversial? Often, controversies arise when most people agree that there is a problem, but people disagree about the best way to solve the problem. There is little argument that poverty is a major problem in the United States, especially in inner cities and rural areas. Yet, people disagree vehemently about the best way to address the problem. To some, the answer is social programs, such as welfare, food stamps, and public housing. However, many argue that such subsidies encourage dependence on government benefits while unfairly penalizing those who work and pay taxes, and that the real solution is to require people to support themselves.

American society is in a constant state of change, and sometimes modern practices clash with what many consider to be "traditional values," which are often rooted in conservative political views or religious beliefs. Many blame high crime rates, and problems such as poverty, illiteracy, and drug use on the breakdown of the traditional family structure of a married mother and father raising their children. Since the "sexual revolution" of the 1960s and 1970s, sparked in part by the widespread availability of the birth control pill, marriage rates have declined, and the number of children born outside of marriage has increased. The sexual revolution led to controversies over birth control, sex education, and other issues, most prominently abortion. Similarly, the gay rights movement has been challenged as a threat to traditional values. While many gay men and lesbians want to have the same right to marry and raise families as heterosexuals, many politicians and others have challenged gay marriage and adoption as a threat to American society.

Sometimes, new technology raises issues that we have never faced before, and society disagrees about the best solution. Are people free to swap music online, or does this violate the copyright laws that protect songwriters and musicians' ownership of the music that they create? Should scientists use "genetic engineering" to create new crops that are resistant to disease and pests and produce more food, or is it too risky to use a laboratory to create plants that nature never intended? Modern medicine has continued to increase the average lifespan—which is now 77 years, up from under 50 years at the beginning of the twentieth century—but many people are now choosing to die in comfort rather than living with painful ailments in their later years. For doctors, this presents an ethical dilemma: should they allow their patients to die? Should they assist patients in ending their own lives painlessly?

Perhaps the most controversial issues are those that implicate a Constitutional right. The Bill of Rights—the first 10 Amendments to the U.S. Constitution—spell out some of the most fundamental rights that distinguish our democracy from other nations with fewer freedoms. However, the sparsely worded document is open to interpretation, with each side saying that the Constitution is on their side. The Bill of Rights was meant to protect individual liberties; however, the needs of some individuals clash with society's needs. Thus, the Constitution often serves as a battleground between individuals and government officials seeking to protect society in some way. The First Amendment's guarantee of "freedom of speech" leads to some very difficult questions. Some forms of expression—such as burning an American flag—lead to public outrage, but are protected by the First Amendment. Other types of expression that most people find objectionable—such as child pornography—are not protected by the Constitution. The question is not only where to draw the line, but whether drawing lines around constitutional rights threatens our liberty.

The Bill of Rights raises many other questions about individual rights and societal "good." Is a prayer before a high school football game an "establishment of religion" prohibited by the First Amendment? Does the Second Amendment's promise of "the right to bear arms" include concealed handguns? Does stopping and frisking someone standing on a known drug corner constitute "unreasonable search and seizure" in violation of the Fourth Amendment? Although the U.S. Supreme Court has the ultimate authority in interpreting the U.S. Constitution, their answers do not always satisfy the public. When a group of nine people—sometimes by a five-to-four vote—makes a decision that affects hundreds of millions of others, public outcry can be expected. For example, the Supreme Court's 1973 ruling in *Roe v. Wade* that abortion is protected by the Constitution did little to quell the debate over abortion.

Whatever the root of the controversy, the books in the POINT-COUNTERPOINT series seek to explain to the reader the origins of the debate, the current state of the law, and the arguments on either side of the debate. Our hope in creating this series is that the reader will be better informed about the issues facing not only our politicians, but all of our nation's citizens, and become more actively involved in resolving these debates, as voters, concerned citizens, journalists, or maybe even elected officials.

While most of the previous volumes in this series have focused primarily on the legal and political aspects of current controversies, this volume takes a deeper look at the science behind one of the most controversial issues of our time: global warming. Many of the nations with which the United States is usually allied have taken international action to reduce "greenhouse gases," which help the atmosphere retain heat. The United States, however, has not signed the treaty known as the Kyoto Protocol.

Many politicians have criticized the federal government for failing to act, most notably, former vice president Al Gore. Proponents of action say that the Earth is warming at an alarming rate, as a direct result of human activity, and that action to correct the problem is long overdue. However, during his eight years in office, President George W. Bush opposed mandatory regulations on global warming, as did many other elected officials. Restrictions on greenhouse gases, opponents say, interfere with necessary and desirable activities such as transportation, manufacturing, and construction; therefore, they believe that joining the Kyoto Protocol would harm the U.S. economy. Many opponents also dispute some of the science touted by environmental activists, arguing that the Earth's temperature has naturally fluctuated over the millennia and questioning the level of harm that global warming can cause. This volume presents some of the scientific and economic arguments used by both sides in the debate, helping the reader to form an opinion on this pressing issue.

The Problem of Global Warming

I n 2007, the Norwegian Nobel Committee recognized global warming as an international concern. In October of that year, it awarded the Nobel Peace Prize to former vice president Al Gore and the Intergovernmental Panel on Climate Change (IPCC), an agency of the United Nations (UN). Its prize announcement said:

> Through the scientific reports it has issued over the past two decades, the IPCC has created an ever-broader informed consensus about the connection between human activities and global warming. Thousands of scientists and officials from over one hundred countries have collaborated to achieve greater certainty as to the scale of the warming. . . .
>
> Al Gore has for a long time been one of the world's leading environmentalist politicians. He became aware at an early

stage of the climatic challenges the world is facing. His strong commitment, reflected in political activity, lectures, films and books, has strengthened the struggle against climate change. He is probably the single individual who has done most to create greater worldwide understanding of the measures that need to be adopted.[1]

Emphasizing the seriousness of the issue, the committee warned: "Action is necessary now, before climate change moves beyond man's control."[2]

The Industrial Revolution, the Automobile, and Fossil Fuels

For most of the time humans have been on the Earth, our energy consumption was modest. Our ancestors burned readily available materials, like wood and animal dung, to provide heat and light. However, energy-usage patterns changed dramatically beginning with the Industrial Revolution, which began in the late eighteenth century. A Scottish engineer named James Watt improved the design of the steam engine, making it efficient enough to power machinery. The steam engine was followed by the locomotive and steamship, which made it easier to transport coal to factories. Coal powered a variety of new machines that could do much more work than humans or animals. Watt's steam engine triggered far-reaching economic and social changes, and it had a dramatic impact on the planet itself.

By 1820, the worldwide transition to coal was well underway. However, the smoke and smog coming from burning coal had a serious downside: "[C]ity-dwellers began to die prematurely from a new pestilence. London's air quickly became so bad that by 1879–80, some three thousand were killed by aggravated lung conditions. Indeed, by the time the political will was found to ban coal-burning domestic hearths in the mid-1950s, lung ailments had killed more Londoners than even the 1918 influenza pandemic."[3]

At the time, people had no idea that the burning of coal released yet another pollutant into the atmosphere—a colorless, odorless gas called carbon dioxide (CO_2), which scientists now call the biggest contributor to global warming.

In the mid-nineteenth century, coal gave way to oil as the fuel of choice. Even though humans had known about oil for centuries, they had made limited use of it until this time. After the drilling of an oil well in Pennsylvania in 1859, oil gained widespread acceptance as a source of energy. That was soon followed by the automobile. In 1876, Nikolaus Otto built an internal combustion engine capable of powering a passenger car. Others improved on Otto's design, and before long, the internal combustion engine became the largest single factor in making petroleum a key source of energy. Mass production made automobiles more affordable, and millions of people bought them. Today, there are more than 500 million cars and trucks worldwide, and an entire way of life has developed around the automobile—and the internal combustion engine that powers it. However, oil-burning automobiles, like coal-burning factories, released pollutants into the air—and those pollutants include carbon dioxide.

Greenhouse Gases and the "Greenhouse Effect"

Both coal and oil contain carbon. It is not only one of the most plentiful elements on Earth but also essential to living things. Green plants use the Sun's energy to turn carbon dioxide and water into simple sugars, called carbohydrates. Many animals eat those plants for nutrition, and ultimately, human beings eat both the plants and the animals that eat them.

Some plants and animals—and the carbon they contained— got trapped beneath the Earth's surface and eventually became the coal and oil we burn. Authors Peter Huber and Mark Mills explain: "Eight hundred million years ago, the Earth's air was mostly carbon dioxide. Green plants evolved and flourished in

(continues on page 16)

Important Dates Relating to Global Warming

c. 1784
The Industrial Revolution begins after James Watt invents a version of the steam engine that would later be put to use in mines and factories.

1859
A team of men led by Edwin L. Drake, an oil company executive, drills an oil well near Titusville, Pennsylvania. Drake's well leads to the development of a large and powerful oil industry in America.

1876
Nikolaus Otto, a German inventor, builds an internal combustion engine capable of powering an automobile. Otto's former business partner, Gottlieb Daimler, later improves on Otto's design.

1896
Svante Arrhenius, a Swedish chemist, publishes a paper in which he argues that humans' consumption of fossil fuels has the potential to raise the temperature of the atmosphere.

1937
Glen Thomas Trewartha, a professor at the University of Wisconsin, uses the phrase "greenhouse effect" in his textbook on weather and climate.

1958
Roger Revelle, a researcher at the Scripps Institution of Oceanography, begins taking measurements of the atmosphere's carbon dioxide concentration atop Mauna Kea in Hawaii. His work eventually demonstrates that greenhouse gas emissions by humans contribute to the greenhouse effect.

1978
Congress enacts the National Climate Act, which directs the president to establish a program to understand and respond to human-caused climate change. President Jimmy Carter, in turn, asks the National Research Council to investigate global warming. The NRC issues a report that warns of the possibility of significant climate change if the world continues its "business-as-usual" approach.

1987
Congress enacts the Global Climate Protection Act, which directs the Environmental Protection Agency to propose a "coordinated national policy on global climate change." That legislation also expresses lawmakers' finding that "ongoing pollution and deforestation may be contributing now to an irreversible process."

1987
Twenty-four countries sign the Montreal Protocol on Substances That Deplete the Ozone Layer. The treaty, which has since been signed by nearly every country, is the first international agreement to address a serious threat to the Earth's environment.

1988
On June 23, climatologist James Hansen of the National Aeronautics and Space Administration warns a congressional panel that the Earth's temperature is rising and that human activity is causing it.

1988
Delegates from nearly 50 countries meet at the First International Conference on the Changing Atmosphere. That fall, the Intergovernmental Panel on Climate Change (IPCC) is formed under the auspices of the United Nations.

1990
The IPCC releases its *First Assessment Report* on climate change. It suggests that human activity is causing global warming and that higher greenhouse gas concentrations will increase the Earth's temperature.

1992
The Earth Summit is held at Rio de Janeiro, Brazil. Delegates from more than 170 countries sign the UN Framework Convention on Climate Change (UNFCCC), which commits the international community to stabilizing greenhouse gas concentrations. However, the UNFCCC contains no binding measures.

1995
The IPCC releases its *Second Assessment Report*, which finds that "the balance of evidence suggests a discernible human influence on global climate."

(continues)

(continued)

1996

Delegates from countries that signed the UNFCCC conclude that the Earth's temperature should not be allowed to rise by more than about 3.6°F (2°C) above its pre–Industrial Revolution level, and the atmosphere's carbon dioxide concentration should not exceed 550 parts per million.

1997

Delegates from more than 170 countries agree to the Kyoto Protocol, which obligates industrialized countries to reduce their carbon dioxide emissions by 5.2 percent by 2012. Earlier that year, however, the United States Senate unanimously expressed its opposition to the treaty unless it covered developing countries as well. The Kyoto Protocol is never sent to the Senate for ratification.

2001

President George W. Bush announces that the United States would not agree to the Kyoto Protocol.

2001

The IPCC releases its *Third Assessment Report*. It finds stronger evidence that most of the warming observed during the previous 50 years is the result of human activities and warns of potentially huge global temperature increases by the end of the twenty-first century unless greenhouse gas emissions are reduced.

2003

Senators John McCain of Arizona and Joe Lieberman of Connecticut sponsor legislation that would set limits on industrial greenhouse gases. The proposal contains a cap-and-trade system: companies that meet emissions targets can sell "credits" to companies that fail to meet them. The bill is defeated in the Senate.

(continued from page 13)

profusion and sucked up most of it. Some of the plants sank into swamps, and then sank deeper. Hence the fossil fuels that we now burn in such quantities."[4]

When fossil fuels are burned, the carbon they contain combines with oxygen to form carbon dioxide. That carbon dioxide

2004

With Russia's agreement to join the Kyoto Protocol, the treaty has support from countries responsible for 55 percent of the industrialized world's emissions. It takes effect in February 2005.

2006

In *Massachusetts v. Environmental Protection Agency*, the U.S. Supreme Court holds that the Environmental Protection Agency violated the Clean Air Act by refusing to investigate whether carbon dioxide is a "pollutant" within the meaning of the act.

2006

An Inconvenient Truth, a documentary featuring former vice president Al Gore, warns of the consequences of unchecked global warming. It later receives the Academy Award for Best Documentary (Feature).

2007

On January 1, the California Global Warming Solutions Act takes effect. It requires a reduction of the state's greenhouse gas emissions to 1990 levels by the year 2020 and authorizes the creation of a cap-and-trade system as one means of achieving that goal.

2007

The IPCC releases its *Fourth Assessment Report*, which calls the evidence of global warming "unequivocal" and concludes that humans are "very likely" responsible for higher temperatures. Later that year, the IPCC and Al Gore are named joint winners of the Nobel Peace Prize for their work in publicizing the threat of global warming.

2012

The Kyoto Protocol's emissions limits are scheduled to expire.

is released into the atmosphere, where it joins the carbon dioxide that results from natural processes such as the decaying of organic matter and the breathing of animals. Most of it is absorbed by the Earth's oceans, trees and other plants, and the soil. However, when more carbon dioxide is released than the Earth can absorb, it accumulates in the atmosphere.

During the 1820s, a French scientist named Jean-Baptiste-Joseph Fourier observed: "The atmosphere acts like a hothouse, because it lets through the light rays of the sun but retains the dark rays from the ground."[5] The phrase "greenhouse effect" was later coined to describe this phenomenon, and carbon dioxide and other heat-trapping gases were given the name "greenhouse gases." Toward the end of the nineteenth century, Swedish chemist Svante Arrhenius published an article in which he said that industrial pollution in the atmosphere would raise temperatures on Earth:

> Two gases—water vapor and CO_2—are responsible for the warming of Earth's atmosphere. Because they are transparent to light emitted by the Sun, its rays pass through and strike the planet. The light is largely absorbed and reemitted at Earth's surface as infrared radiation, or heat, invisible to the naked eye. Due to its altered wavelength, the infrared radiation cannot pass back through the water vapor and CO_2 as before. Some of it is absorbed, and part of what is absorbed is radiated back toward Earth's surface, thus trapping heat and warming the planet.[6]

In 1938, a British coal engineer named George S. Callendar published what proved to be a prophetic article. Callendar determined that the Earth's temperature had risen during the previous 50 years, and that it would continue to rise because the end of industrial output was nowhere in sight and so much pollution was already in the atmosphere. Callendar did not consider greenhouse gas emissions a threat, and neither did Arrhenius. In fact, both men believed that global warming would benefit humanity by making winters less harsh. Up to a point, they were right. Bjorn Lomborg, a professor at the Copenhagen Business School, explains that "if the atmosphere did not contain greenhouse gases, the average temperature on the Earth would be approximately 59°F colder, and it is unlikely that life as we know it would be able to exist."[7]

Global Warming Becomes a Concern

Some 50 years ago, scientists began to recognize the dangers of global warming. One of the first published warnings appeared in the journal *Tellus* in 1957. Roger Revelle and Hans Suess, two oceanographers at the Scripps Institute in California, concluded that "human beings are now carrying out a large scale geophysical experiment of a kind that could not have happened in the past nor be reproduced in the future. Within a few centuries we are returning to the atmosphere and oceans the concentrated organic carbon stored in sedimentary rocks over hundreds of millions of years."[8] Al Gore argues that Revelle was years ahead of his time: "He saw clearly that the global, post-World War II economic expansion, driven by explosive population growth and fueled mainly by coal and oil, was likely to produce an unprecedented and dangerous increase in the amount of CO_2 in the Earth's atmosphere."[9]

By the 1970s, scientists expressed concern over the possibility that global warming could trigger droughts, floods, and other disasters. Policy makers, too, started to pay attention. In 1978, Congress enacted the National Climate Act, which directed the president to establish a program to help Americans understand the implications of climate change. President Jimmy Carter, in turn, asked the National Research Council (NRC) to investigate global warming. In its report, the NRC said that human activity could result in substantial climate change and warned: "A wait-and-see policy may mean waiting until it is too late."[10]

In this country, global warming became a matter of serious concern to policy makers in 1988. On June 23 of that year, a day when the temperature in Washington, D.C., topped 100°F (38°C), National Aeronautics and Space Administration (NASA) climatologist James Hansen offered startling testimony to a U.S. Senate committee, according to Brian Fagan:

Hansen had impressive data from 2,000 weather stations around the world, which documented not only a century-long warming trend but a sharp resumption of warming after the early 1970s. Four of the warmest years of the past 130 had occurred in the 1980s. The first five months of 1988 had brought the highest temperatures yet. Hansen flatly proclaimed that the earth was warming on a permanent basis because of humanity's promiscuous use of fossil fuels. Furthermore, the world could expect a much higher frequency of heat waves, droughts, and other extreme climatic events. His predictions thrust global warming into the public arena almost overnight.[11]

The World Community Takes Action

At about the same time that Hansen testified on Capitol Hill, global warming also gained the international community's attention. In 1988, the United Nations created the IPCC to find out whether the Earth was growing warmer because of the natural variability of the climate or because of human activities. Two years later, the IPCC released its *First Assessment Report* on climate change. It concluded that activities such as industrialization and the use of gasoline-powered vehicles had caused greenhouse gas concentrations to increase and that the Earth's temperature had risen by 0.5°F to 1°F (0.3°C to 0.6°C) over the past 100 years. The panel refused, however, to rule out the possibility that the warming was the result of natural variability rather than human activity. In the years that followed, the IPCC issued three more assessment reports. Each concluded with greater certainty that the Earth was getting warmer, the warming was the result of higher greenhouse gas concentrations, and human beings were responsible for emitting those gases.

Convinced that global warming threatened the planet, world leaders took steps to combat it. In 1992, delegates representing more than 170 countries—including the United States—attended the Earth Summit at Rio de Janeiro, where they agreed to the

Above, a photo of heavy traffic in thick smog in China. Although good air quality is a worldwide concern, air pollution levels in Beijing on an average day are almost five times greater than the World Health Organization's standards for safety.

UN Framework Convention on Climate Change (UNFCCC). That document committed its signers to stabilize greenhouse gas concentrations at a level that would prevent dangerous human interference with the Earth's climate. It contained no binding measures, however. In December 1997, after seeing little progress on reducing emissions, the countries that signed the UNFCCC met in Kyoto, Japan, to forge an agreement that would *require* countries to reduce their emissions. The Kyoto Protocol obligated 37 industrialized nations, including the United States, to cut their combined emissions by an average of 5.2 percent by 2012. An important feature of Kyoto was something known as emissions trading: "Under this mechanism, the nations of the world agree on an overall, total cap for carbon emissions. Then countries that exceed that cap can buy credits from countries that do not exceed it. For instance, the United States (or big carbon emitters

The Kyoto Protocol

In 1992, most countries signed the United Nations Framework Convention on Climate Change (UNFCCC), which is considered a major step forward in addressing the problem of global warming. Article 2 of the UNFCCC states:

> The ultimate objective of this Convention and any related legal instruments that the Conference of the Parties may adopt is to achieve, in accordance with the relevant provisions of the Convention, stabilisation of greenhouse gas concentrations in the atmosphere at a level that would prevent dangerous anthropogenic [human-caused] interference with the climate system. Such a level should be achieved within a time frame sufficient to allow ecosystems to adapt naturally to climate change, to ensure that food production is not threatened and to enable economic development to proceed in a sustainable manner.

What constitutes "dangerous anthropogenic interference with the climate system" is a value judgment. Experts disagree as to how high greenhouse gas concentrations can rise—and how long they can remain there—without creating the risk of runaway global warming.

Even though most of the world agreed to the UNFCCC, it became increasingly obvious to member countries that only a binding commitment by developed countries to reduce their emissions would send a signal strong enough to persuade businesses and individuals to take the issue seriously. As a result, member countries of the UNFCCC began negotiations on what we now call the Kyoto Protocol.

After lengthy negotiations, delegates at the Third Conference of the Parties (COP) approved the Kyoto Protocol at their meeting in Kyoto, Japan, in 1997. The COP is the supreme body of the UNFCCC. Among other things, it oversees compliance with the Kyoto Protocol and reviews the evidence about global warming with a view toward future climate policy. Even after the Kyoto Protocol expires in 2012, the COP—as well as the UNFCCC itself—will continue to exist. Thus it is possible that the international community will someday agree to a new treaty that replaces Kyoto.

within the United States) could pay to protect and expand forests in Central America to absorb some of the excess carbon dioxide emitted inside the United States."[12]

Because it affects virtually every major sector of the economy, Kyoto is considered the most far-reaching environmental treaty ever adopted. For the same reasons, however, it was necessary for delegates to draw up a politically acceptable document. Most observers consider Kyoto a compromise; it has been criticized on one hand for setting unworkable targets over too short a time frame and on the other for doing too little to stop the accumulation of greenhouse gases.

Kyoto requires "Annex I" countries (37 industrialized countries, including the United States, the European Union, and the former East Bloc) to implement policies aimed at improving energy efficiency and reducing greenhouse gas emissions. Those countries must meet an overall target of a 5.2 percent reduction in greenhouse gas emissions by 2012. (That target is measured relative to 1990 emissions levels.) Annex I countries bear the burden of reducing emissions for two reasons: They can better afford the cost of doing so, and they have been responsible for most of the emissions. Emissions-reduction targets vary by country; for example, it is 7 percent for the United States, 6 percent for Canada and Japan, and 8 percent for the European Union. Because compliance is based on *net* changes in emissions, a country can offset its emissions by taking steps such as planting trees, which absorb carbon dioxide.

To give countries flexibility in meeting their emissions-reduction targets, Kyoto offers three market-based options. One is emissions trading: countries that emit less carbon dioxide than the target or take steps to capture carbon dioxide (for example, by expanding forests) can sell "credits" to those countries whose emissions exceed the target. Countries can also earn credits by implementing emissions-reduction projects, either at home or in other countries, or by transferring clean-energy technology to or making investments in developing countries.

Even though Kyoto was signed in 1997, it did not take effect until the 90th day after at least 55 countries, including Annex I countries that accounted for at least 55 percent of that group's carbon dioxide emissions, agreed to its terms. That did not happen until Russia agreed to Kyoto on November 18, 2004, making the treaty's effective date February 16, 2005.

Source: UNFCCC Kyoto Protocol Page. http://unfccc.int/kyoto_protocol/items/2830.php.

Because of strong opposition in Congress and the White House, the United States never agreed to Kyoto. The United States is not always in agreement with the United Nations; in fact, many Americans are calling for the United States to stop allowing other nations to interfere with its sovereignty.

Are Humans Changing the Earth's Climate?

The most contentious issue related to global warming is whether it is the result of human activity. That issue, in turn, is complicated by the nature of climate—that is, the slowly varying

James Hansen Testifies About Global Warming

On June 23, 1988, climatologist James Hansen, the head of NASA's Goddard Institute of Space Studies, testified about global warming before a U.S. Senate committee. Hansen was the first leading climate scientist to tell the public that temperatures had risen beyond the limits of natural variability—in other words, that human-caused global warming had begun. Below are some highlights of his testimony:

> I would like to draw three main conclusions. Number one, the earth is warmer in 1988 than at any time in the history of instrumental measurements. Number two, the global warming is now large enough that we can ascribe with a high degree of confidence a cause and effect relationship to the greenhouse effect. And number three, our computer climate simulations indicate that the greenhouse effect is already large enough to begin to effect [sic] the probability of extreme events such as summer heat waves.
>
> The present temperature is the highest in the period of record. The rate of warming in the past 25 years … is the highest on record. The four warmest years … have all been in the 1980s. And 1988 so far is so much warmer than 1987.
>
> Casual association requires first that the warming be larger than natural climate variability and, second, that the magnitude and nature of the warming be consistent with the greenhouse mechanism. … The observed

aspects of the Earth's atmosphere, oceans, and landmasses. Long before the Industrial Revolution, the climate had undergone a series of dramatic changes. John Carlisle, the director of the Environmental Policy Task Force, explains:

> Over the last 700,000 years, the climate has operated on a relatively predictable schedule of 100,000-year glaciation cycles. Each glaciation cycle is typically characterized by 90,000 years of cooling, an ice age, followed by an abrupt warming period, called an interglacial, which lasts 10,000–12,000 years. The

warming during the past 30 years ... is almost 0.4 degrees Centigrade by 1987 relative to climatology, which is defined as the 30 year mean, 1950 to 1980 and, in fact, the warming is more than 0.4 degrees Centigrade in 1988. The probability of a chance warming of that magnitude is about 1 percent. So, with 99 percent confidence we can state that the warming during this time period is a real warming trend.

Altogether the evidence is that the earth is warming by an amount that is too large to be a chance fluctuation and the similarity of the warming to that expected from the greenhouse effect represents a very strong case in my opinion, that the greenhouse effect has been detected and it is changing our climate now.

Then my third point.... A hot summer is defined as the hottest one-third of summers in the 1950 to 1980 period, which is the period the Weather Bureau uses for defining climatology. So, in that period the probability of having a hot summer was 33 percent, but by the 1990s [sic], you can see that the greenhouse effect has increased the probability of a hot summer to somewhere between 55 and 70 percent in Washington according to our climate model simulations.

I believe that this change in the frequency of hot summers is large enough to be noticeable to the average person. So, we have already reached a point that the greenhouse effect is important.

Source: Statement of James Hansen to the Senate Committee on Energy and Natural Resources, June 23, 1988.

last ice age reached its coolest point 18,000 to 20,000 years ago when the average temperature was 9–12.6°F cooler than present. Earth is currently in a warm interglacial called the Holocene that began 10,700 years ago.[13]

Even in the last 10,000 years, which has been a period of relatively stable climate, temperatures have varied considerably. Carlisle explains:

> During the Holocene, there have been about seven major warming and cooling trends, some lasting as long as 3000 years, others as short as 650. Most interesting of all, however, is that the temperature variation in many of these periods averaged as much as 1.8°F, .3°F more than the temperature increase of the last 150 years. Furthermore, of the six major temperature variations occurring prior to the current era, three produced temperatures warmer than the present average temperature of 59°F while three produced cooler temperatures.[14]

About 1,000 years ago, the Earth experienced the Medieval Warm Period. That was followed by a centuries-long period during which temperatures were considerably colder than they are now. In fact, the era between 1650 and 1850 is sometimes referred to as the "Little Ice Age." Temperatures recovered during the twentieth century, and a strong warming trend, which continues to this day, began during the 1970s.

The Debate Continues

Global warming is not only a matter of worldwide concern but has become a subject of intense debate in this country. Activists, led by Al Gore, believe that it poses a threat to humans unlike any we have faced before. They view the Kyoto Protocol as the first step in a long-term strategy to reduce emissions to a safe level before climate change becomes uncontrollable. However, some scientists and many policy makers are unconvinced. In their view, the IPCC rushed to judgment in blaming global warming on humans. These critics also contend that Kyoto-type solutions would cause more damage than global warming itself, and that we should address more pressing problems than the future effects of climate change—which may never materialize.

Opponents consider the Kyoto Protocol unfair to industrialized countries, especially the United States, because it does nothing to limit the emissions of developing countries, including China and India. They also contend that Kyoto would cripple the industrialized world's economies, while having little effect on global temperatures. The same forces that led the effort to keep this country out of Kyoto also oppose mandatory emissions limits in general and so far have stopped climate legislation in Congress. Thus the debate over how to fight global warming—including whether we should act at all—will continue.

Summary

Most scientists believe that the Earth has grown warmer and blame it primarily on the accumulation of carbon dioxide in the atmosphere—much of which is the result of humans burning coal and oil. Recent changes to the Earth's climate, and the likelihood of even larger changes in the years to come, have convinced world leaders to take action. The international community has committed itself to reducing greenhouse gas emissions. Most industrialized countries have signed the Kyoto Protocol, which obligates them to reduce emissions. However, opposition to Kyoto was so strong in this country that the United States refused to join it. Despite considerable evidence that humans are changing the Earth's climate, many of our public officials still oppose measures that would force us to scale back our use of fossil fuels. Consequently, global warming is likely to remain the subject of intense debate.

Human Activity Causes Global Warming

F or years, there have been clear signs of a profound change in the climate. In 2004, author Ross Gelbspan wrote:

> The evidence is not subtle. It is apparent in the trickling melt-water from the glaciers in the Andes Mountains that will soon leave many people on Bolivia's mountainside villages with no water to irrigate their crops and, after that, not even enough to drink. It is visible in the rising waters of the Pacific Ocean that recently prompted the prime minister of New Zealand to offer a haven to the residents of the island nation of Tuvalu as it slowly goes under. It is evident in the floods that, in 2002, inundated whole cities in Germany, Russia, and the Czech Republic. It is underscored in the United States by the spread of West Nile virus to forty-two states—and to 230 species of birds, insects, and animals—and in the record-setting 412

tornadoes that leveled whole towns during a ten-day span in May 2003.[1]

There is growing evidence that the climate is changing, and that the accumulation of greenhouse gases is bringing this about. As a result, many believe there is no longer any doubt that humans are causing global warming.

Global temperatures are rising.

In 2001, the Intergovernmental Panel on Climate Change (IPCC) reported that global temperatures were about 1°F (0.6°C) higher than they were 100 years earlier. The rise in temperatures has been especially sharp in recent years. According to the IPCC, 11 of the 12 warmest years since 1850—about the time it became common practice to keep temperature records—occurred between 1995 and 2006.

Even though a 1°F (0.6°C) increase seems insignificant, it has been blamed for extreme weather, which could be getting worse. Ross Gelbspan remarked: "One of the first signs of early stage global warming is an increase in weather extremes—longer droughts, more heat waves, more severe storms, and much more intense, severe dumps of rain and snow. Today, extreme weather events constitute a much larger portion of news budgets than they did twenty years ago."[2]

Scientists have tried to determine whether recent temperature increases are the result of natural variations in the climate. Increasingly, the answer appears to be "no." In 1998, Michael Mann, Raymond Bradley, and Malcolm Hughes reconstructed from tree rings, ice cores, and sediments the history of the global climate over the previous 1,000 years and published their findings in the journal *Geophysical Research Letters*. According to Gelbspan: "Their research . . . showed that from about the year 1,000 to the mid-nineteenth century, the climate was actually cooling very slightly—about one-fourth of a degree. But in the

(continues on page 32)

Global Warming Words and Phrases

Adaptation. Measures that reduce our vulnerability to the effects of global warming but do not address the causes of global warming itself. An example of adaptation is building barriers that will hold back surges of seawater during severe storms caused by changing climate.

Aerosols. Atmospheric particles produced by the burning of fossil fuels, especially coal. Many scientists believe that during the mid-twentieth century, before governments enforced clean-air laws, aerosols in the atmosphere blocked some of the Sun's radiation and that this so-called global dimming temporarily offset the warming caused by greenhouse gases.

Albedo. A measure of surface reflectivity, commonly expressed as a number between 0 and 1. Light-colored objects such as Arctic sea ice have a high albedo, while darker-colored objects such as ocean water have a lower albedo. Scientists believe that the melting of sea ice will result in solar radiation bring absorbed rather than reflected, which will, in turn, add to the problem of global warming.

Anthropogenic. Caused by humans. In the debate over global warming, the most contentious issue is whether recent changes in climate are the result of human activity rather than natural variations.

Atlantic conveyor. A pattern of ocean currents by which the Atlantic Ocean moves warm water from the tropics to more northerly latitudes. The Gulf Stream, which moderates the climate of western Europe, is part of it. Some scientists fear that higher ocean temperatures could have the paradoxical effect of slowing, or even shutting down, the Atlantic conveyor and sending much of Europe into a mini ice age.

Cap-and-trade. A flexible means of regulating emissions. Regulators set the maximum allowable amount that can be emitted, which is called the "cap," and then distribute "allowances" to companies that emit the pollutant. Those companies that can easily reduce their emissions can trade their extra allowances to companies that lack the money or technology to reduce theirs. Cap-and-trade is a key feature of the Kyoto Protocol.

Carbon cycle. Human beings and animals breathe in oxygen and exhale carbon dioxide. Conversely, plants take in carbon dioxide and release oxygen. Living plants, such as trees, store significant amounts of carbon dioxide while they are alive. The oceans and the Earth's soil also store carbon dioxide.

Carbon dioxide. The fourth most abundant gas in the atmosphere. It makes up less than 0.04 percent of all the gases in the atmosphere, up from 0.028 percent in the pre-industrial era. Scientists believe that the accumulation of carbon dioxide in the atmosphere is the leading cause of global warming.

Carbon tax. A tax levied on fossil fuels. Many proposals start with a relatively modest tax, for example, $10 per ton of carbon emitted, with the tax rising in future years as emissions limits become more stringent. In theory, both a carbon tax and a cap-and-trade system force emitters to become more accountable for their contribution to global warming.

Climate. The pattern or cycle of weather conditions, such as temperature and precipitation, occurring over a large area and averaged over many years. Many scientists believe that it takes decades or more to evaluate climate trends.

Climate change. Measurable changes in either the mean or the variability of the properties of climate (temperature, for instance) that persists for an extended period of time. Some experts use the term to refer to any change in climate over time, while others use it to refer only to those changes that result from human activity.

El Niño. A warming of the ocean surface off the western coast of South America that has occurred every 4 to 12 years. It is one of the most powerful influences on the world's weather. El Niño affects Pacific jet stream winds, alters storm tracks, and creates unusual—and often destructive—weather in various parts of the world. In recent years, El Niños have become more frequent and more intense; some scientists believe this is the result of global warming.

Feedback loop. A phenomenon in which rising temperatures change the environment in ways that create even more heat. Scientists consider feedback loops the biggest threat resulting from global warming because they could set off an uncontrollable climatic chain reaction.

(continues)

(continued)

Forcing. A factor that can cause a change in the climate by affecting the Earth's energy balance.

Fossil fuel. A naturally occurring carbon-containing material that, when burned, produces heat or energy. Fossil fuels include coal, oil, and natural gas.

Greenhouse gases. Gases that trap heat radiation in the Earth's atmosphere. Of those gases, carbon dioxide is the greatest concern because its increasing presence in the atmosphere has been blamed for much of man-made warming. Other greenhouse gases include chlorofluorocarbon, methane, nitrous oxide, and water vapor.

Greenhouse theory. The theory that human emissions of greenhouse gases are heating the Earth beyond the limits of past climate variation and thus endangering its ecosystems.

Ice age. A long period during which the Earth's temperature decreases, resulting in an expansion of the polar ice sheets and mountain glaciers. The most recent ice age ended about 20,000 years ago. At one point, a 2-mile-thick (3.2-kilometer) sheet of ice covered much of the Upper Midwest and Great Lakes region of this country.

Interglacial periods. Periods between ice ages that are about 10,000 years in duration. Some scientists believe that the Earth is overdue for another ice age, and that it may arrive suddenly.

Kyoto Protocol. An agreement that obligates the world's industrialized nations to reduce their emissions of carbon dioxide and five other greenhouse gases. The U.S. Senate never ratified the treaty.

Mitigation. Measures aimed at reducing greenhouse gas emissions in order to make future global warming less severe. Mitigation and adaptation

(continued from page 29)

last 150 years, beginning with the widespread industrialization of the late nineteenth century, the temperature has shot upward at a rate unseen in the last 10,000 years."[3] Their so-called hockey stick graph figured prominently in the IPCC's *Third Assessment Report*, released in 2001, and supported the panel's finding that there was "a discernible human influence" on the Earth's climate.

are the two major strategies for dealing with global warming, and both can be pursued at the same time.

Modern Warming. A warming trend that began in the second half of the 1800s after centuries of below-normal temperatures. After a significant warming that occurred between 1920 and 1940, scientists looked at the possibility that we were experiencing a change in the climate itself rather than simple variations in the climate.

No-regrets measures. Measures whose benefits, such as more fuel-efficient automobiles or factories that emit less pollution, equal or exceed their costs. These measures are attractive to governments wanting to mitigate global warming.

Paleoclimate. Climate as it existed in the distant past. Because systematic climate records were not kept before the nineteenth century, scientists rely on proxy measurements, such as their analysis of ice cores and tree rings, to reconstruct the climate as it existed tens or even hundreds of thousands of years ago.

Solar irradiance. The amount of visible, infrared, and ultraviolet light from the Sun that arrives on the Earth's surface during a given time period. Solar irradiance varies slightly over solar cycles. Some scientists insist that these changes in solar irradiance have a greater influence on the Earth's temperature than the accumulation of greenhouse gases.

Tipping point. A climate forcing that, if it persists long enough, causes a specific climate-related consequence such as drought or the retreat of glaciers. Somewhere past the tipping point lies the point of no return, beyond which drastic changes to our climate are inevitable, even if the climate forcing is reduced. Some scientists believe that we can pass a tipping point without passing the point of no return.

In its Fourth Assessment Report, the IPCC again sided with Mann and his colleagues. It concluded there were at least 9 chances in 10 that average Northern Hemisphere temperatures were higher during the second half of the twentieth century than during any other 50-year period in the last 500 years, and a better than even chance that they were the highest in at least the past 1,300 years. Turning to the cause of these higher

Polar bears use sea ice as platforms to hunt seals. The International Union for Conservation of Nature and Natural Resources lists global warming as the most significant threat to polar bears, primarily because their sea ice habitat is melting. In 2008, the U.S. Department of the Interior listed polar bears as a threatened species. Some critics, however, suggest that hunters are a greater threat to polar bears.

temperatures, the panel concluded: "The observed widespread warming of the atmosphere and ocean, together with ice mass loss, support the conclusion that it is *extremely unlikely* [less than one chance in 20] that global climate change of the past 50 years can be explained without external forcing and *very likely* [at least nine chances in 10] that it is not due to known natural causes alone."[4]

Greenhouse gas concentrations
are at record levels.

Most scientists agree that the accumulation of greenhouse gases in the atmosphere—carbon dioxide in particular—is one of the primary causes of global warming. The research that led to that finding began about 50 years ago, when Roger Revelle of Harvard University pioneered the measurement of carbon dioxide concentrations. Revelle and his assistant, Charles David Keeling, began taking daily measurements on Mauna Kea in Hawaii. When Revelle began his work, he determined that the carbon dioxide concentration was 315 parts per million (ppm), a little more than 10 percent higher than the pre-Industrial Revolution level of about 280 ppm. Since then, the concentration has steadily crept upward. In 1997, Keeling returned to the global warming debate. He presented a chart showing a steady increase in carbon dioxide concentrations, which had risen to 365 ppm. The "Keeling Curve" was further evidence that humans were causing the Earth's temperature to rise.

In 2007, the IPCC reported that the carbon dioxide concentration stood at 379 ppm—more than one-third higher than when James Watt's first steam engine was placed in service. To put this figure into perspective, the carbon dioxide concentration in Watt's day was well above what it was 20,000 years ago, during the last ice age. Back then, the atmosphere contained only 180 ppm of carbon dioxide. Thus it took almost 20,000 years of the natural workings of climate to increase the carbon dioxide concentration by 100 ppm, but during the industrial age, it took only 100 years for that concentration to increase by another 100 ppm.

Not only has the carbon dioxide concentration increased rapidly, but it has risen to well above what is considered a normal level. In 2007, the IPCC reported: "Global atmospheric concentrations of CO_2, CH_4 [methane] and N_2O [nitrous oxide] have increased markedly as a result of human activities since 1750 and now far exceed pre-industrial values determined from ice cores spanning many thousands of years. . . . The atmospheric concentrations of CO_2 and CH_4 in 2005 exceed by far the natural range over the last 650,000 years."[5]

Emissions and temperatures are likely to keep rising.

Carbon dioxide emissions rose from an estimated 21 billion tons (19 billion metric tons) in 1970 to 38 billion tons (34 billion metric tons) in 2004—an increase of about 80 percent.

The IPCC and Its Assessment Reports

In 1988, the United Nations created the Intergovernmental Panel on Climate Change (IPCC), a scientific body that assembles the world's climate experts to report on the latest scientific findings, to determine whether current global warming was a natural variation in the climate or was due to the activities of human beings.

The IPCC does not do its own research. Instead, more than 800 scientists from over 130 countries around the world read and analyze published scientific data and compile drafts of a so-called assessment report every few years. Some 2,500 other experts review and comment on the report before it is published. In addition, because the IPCC is an intergovernmental body, the report is reviewed by government officials as well as by scientists.

In 1990, the IPCC released its *First Assessment Report*. It found that atmospheric temperatures had increased by 0.5°F to 1°F (0.3°C to 0.6°C) over the past century, and that human activities had substantially increased greenhouse gas concentrations. It also found that increased greenhouse gas concentrations would lead to an additional warming of the Earth's surface. However, the IPCC conceded that uncertainties surrounded its prediction and that higher temperatures might have been the result of natural variability.

The *Second Assessment Report* (1995) found that greenhouse gas concentrations had continued to increase, that the Earth's climate has changed over the past century, and that the balance of evidence suggested "a discernible human influence" on global climate. Even though the panel found that many uncertainties

Furthermore, between 1995 and 2004, emissions grew at twice the rate at which they grew between 1970 and 1994. It is also likely that emissions will continue to increase in the years to come. The IPCC projects that emissions will be 40 to 100 percent higher in 2030 than they were in 2000. It cited a number of factors that would contribute to an increase of this size, including population growth, the cutting down of forests, and higher living standards—and most importantly, even heavier consumption of fossil fuels. Today, about 2.5 billion people still rely on energy sources such as wood and animal dung, and many

remained, it concluded that the increase in global temperatures over the past 100 years was unlikely to have been caused entirely by natural variations. It also found an "emerging pattern of climate response" to humans' emissions of greenhouse gases and substances such as industrial pollutants and concluded that the overall evidence pointed to a human influence on global climate.

The *Third Assessment Report* (2001) concluded that the human contribution to global warming was "greater than originally believed." It determined that the Earth's surface temperature had risen by about 1°F (0.6°C) during the twentieth century and that there was new and stronger evidence that warming over the past 50 years was the result of human activity. The panel warned of potential "large-scale and possibly irreversible changes in Earth systems." It expressed increasing confidence in the ability of climate models—complex computer programs that simulated the Earth's climate—to predict future changes and based on those models, concluded that global temperatures could rise by as much as 10.4°F (5.8°C) by the end of the twenty-first century.

The *Fourth Assessment Report* (2007) concluded that warming of the climate system was "unequivocal" and that most of the temperature increase during the past 50 years was very likely due to increased greenhouse gas resulting from human activities. The report warned of a variety of consequences of continued global warming, including higher ocean levels resulting from the melting of polar ice, droughts and floods, a greater frequency of extreme weather, and even the possibility of large-scale extinction of species and abrupt or irreversible climate change.

The IPCC's *Fifth Assessment Report* is due to be released in 2012 or 2013.

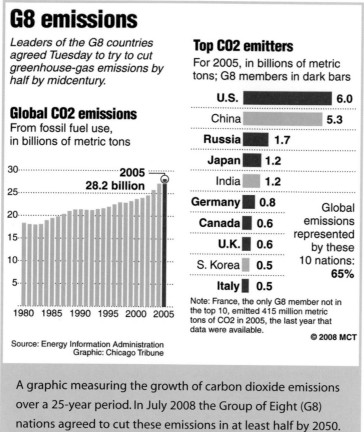

G8 emissions

Leaders of the G8 countries agreed Tuesday to try to cut greenhouse-gas emissions by half by midcentury.

Global CO2 emissions
From fossil fuel use, in billions of metric tons

2005
28.2 billion

1980 1985 1990 1995 2000 2005

Source: Energy Information Administration
Graphic: Chicago Tribune

Top CO2 emitters
For 2005, in billions of metric tons; G8 members in dark bars

U.S.	6.0
China	5.3
Russia	1.7
Japan	1.2
India	1.2
Germany	0.8
Canada	0.6
U.K.	0.6
S. Korea	0.5
Italy	0.5

Global emissions represented by these 10 nations: **65%**

Note: France, the only G8 member not in the top 10, emitted 415 million metric tons of CO2 in 2005, the last year that data were available.

© 2008 MCT

A graphic measuring the growth of carbon dioxide emissions over a 25-year period. In July 2008 the Group of Eight (G8) nations agreed to cut these emissions in at least half by 2050. They also called on the United Nations to help negotiate an emissions agreement with large polluters like India and China, which are not part of the G8.

observers believe that it is only a matter of time before most of these people become consumers of fossil fuels as well. China, in particular, is increasing its use of fossil fuels. Jeffrey Kluger, a *Time* magazine correspondent, wrote: "Between 1990 and 2004, energy consumption rose 37% in India and 53% in China. Beijing is building new coal-fired power plants at the startling rate of one every week. While the most technologically sophisticated coal plants operate at almost 45% efficiency, China's top out at just 33%."[6]

What makes the problem worse yet is the fact that carbon dioxide, once emitted into the atmosphere, can remain there for 100 years or more. Therefore, even if we reduced our greenhouse gas emissions to zero starting today, the gases that we have already released into the atmosphere will affect our climate for decades to come. In 2007, the IPCC found that "past and future anthropogenic [human-caused] CO_2 emissions will continue to contribute to warming and sea level rise for more than a millennium, due to the time scales required for the removal of this gas from the atmosphere."[7] The panel also predicts that the Earth will warm by an additional 0.36°F (0.2°C) during each of the next two decades.

Scientists agree that humans are causing global warming.

In science, there is never complete certainty that a theory is correct. However, there is broad agreement among scientists that the Earth is growing warmer and that human activity is responsible for it. According to Jim Baker, the former head of the National Oceanic and Atmospheric Administration, "There is a better scientific consensus on this issue than any other . . . with the possible exception of Newton's Law of Dynamics."[8]

In 2004, Naomi Oreskes, a science historian at the University of California–San Diego, conducted a survey of articles about global warming. She selected 928 abstracts that had been published in refereed scientific journals between 1993 and 2003 and were listed in a scientific database with the keywords "climate change." Seventy-five percent of those papers accepted the consensus view that human beings were responsible for global warming, and 25 percent took no position on the role played by humans. None disagreed with the consensus position. Oreskes said: "Politicians, economists, journalists, and others may have

(continues on page 42)

Abrupt Climate Change and National Security

In 2002, a National Academy of Sciences report concluded that human activities could trigger an abrupt change in the Earth's climate. One possibility often discussed by scientists is a shutdown of the Gulf Stream, which could cause an abrupt shift to ice age conditions in Europe, possibly within a few years. This has happened before. One shutdown called the Younger Dryas occurred 12,700 years ago. It lasted for about 1,300 years, during which time Britain was covered in permafrost and icebergs appeared as far south as Portugal. A highly exaggerated version of this event provided the basis for the disaster film *The Day After Tomorrow*.

The possibility of abrupt climate change has also attracted the attention of our military. In 2004, *Fortune* magazine reported that strategic planners at the Pentagon had studied the national security implications of a shutdown in the Atlantic conveyor, which, paradoxically, could result from global warming. David Stipp, the *Fortune* reporter, explains: "[W]hen the climate warms, according to the theory, fresh water from melting Arctic glaciers flows into the North Atlantic, lowering the current's salinity—and its density and tendency to sink. A warmer climate also increases rainfall and runoff into the current, further lowering its saltiness. As a result, the conveyor loses its main motive force and can rapidly collapse, turning off the huge heat pump and altering the climate over much of the Northern Hemisphere." The result would be longer, harsher winters; and even worse, serious drought leading to Dust Bowl conditions, wildfires, and a lack of fresh water in parts of the world.

The Pentagon study was headed by Andrew Marshall, an influential Defense Department planner who for more than 30 years headed a secret think tank charged with anticipating future threats to America's national security. Marshall's team prepared an unclassified report, which the Pentagon agreed to share with *Fortune*.

The Pentagon planners envisioned a sudden collapse of the Atlantic conveyor starting in 2010. Its magnitude would be similar to one that occurred about 8,200 years ago, bringing a century of cold, dry, windy weather to the Northern Hemisphere. This collapse is believed to have been triggered by a rise in temperatures similar to today's Modern Warming.

In this vision, the changes in weather are dismissed as "blips" but by 2020, few people doubt that the climate is changing. As temperatures would drop in parts of North America and Europe, severe drought would strike crop-growing regions and violent storms, some powerful enough to break the dikes protecting The Netherlands, would become increasingly common.

The report goes on to note that because of its wealth, crop diversity, and natural resources, the United States would avoid catastrophe. However, this country would also need to fortify its borders to keep out "boat people" and other refugees, make a large investment in nuclear power, and pay steep prices for oil and gas to heat homes and businesses. Europe, which would be especially hard-hit, would have to cope with a flood of refugees—not only from cold countries such as Norway and Sweden but also from drought-stricken regions of Africa.

Effects of the conveyor's collapse would be felt worldwide. China would suffer both drought and flooding as the Asian monsoon becomes less predictable. Millions of Bangladeshis would be forced out of low-lying areas threatened by rising sea levels. Countries with a history of infighting, such as India, would find it difficult to maintain order.

As conditions would continue to deteriorate, the resources and social and economic structures needed to support the Earth's population would come under increasing stress. *Fortune*'s Stipp explained what could happen next: "As the planet's carrying capacity shrinks, an ancient pattern reemerges: the eruption of desperate, all-out wars over food, water, and energy supplies. As Harvard archeologist Steven LeBlanc has noted, wars over resources were the norm until about three centuries ago. When such conflicts broke out, 25% of a population's adult males usually died. As abrupt climate change hits home, warfare may again come to define human life."

In the twenty-first century, such conflicts could be even deadlier. Increased demand for energy would force countries to turn to nuclear energy, and greater concern about their security would lead them to use their nuclear fuel to develop weapons. Desperate, nuclear-armed countries could go to war over refugees or access to cropland and fresh water.

How seriously should our government take threats like this? Stipp answers: "In sum, the risk of abrupt climate change remains uncertain, and it is quite possibly small. But given its dire consequences, it should be elevated beyond a scientific debate. Action now matters, because we may be able to reduce its likelihood of happening, and we can certainly be better prepared if it does. It is time to recognize it as a national security concern."

Source: David Stipp, "Climate Collapse: The Pentagon's Weather Nightmare," *Fortune*, January 26, 2004.

(continued from page 39)
the impression of confusion, disagreement, or discord among climate scientists, but that impression is incorrect."[9]

Scientists are also increasingly confident about the cause of global warming. The IPCC's *Fourth Assessment Report* found: "Warming of the climate system is unequivocal, as is now evident from observations of increases in global average air and ocean temperatures, widespread melting of snow and ice and rising global average sea level."[10] It raised the probability, from at least 66 percent to at least 90 percent, that human beings are responsible for global warming. In the report, the IPCC also found greater reason to be concerned about a range of climate-related events—including extreme weather, higher sea levels, and the impact on vulnerable populations such as residents of the Arctic—than it found in 2001, when it released the *Third Assessment Report*.

Some American policy makers distrust the IPCC because of its affiliation with the United Nations, which some perceive as anti-American. However, the IPCC is not the only scientific body that blames global warming on human activity. After taking office in 2001, President George W. Bush asked the National Academy of Sciences (NAS) to write its own report on global warming. The NAS not only affirmed the IPCC's findings but also indicated that the IPCC might have even understated the magnitude of some coming impacts. In fact, as early as 1992 the NAS had found that the burning of fossil fuels was changing the climate and recommended strong measures to minimize the impact. In addition to the NAS, other U.S. scientific organizations, including the American Meteorological Society, the American Geophysical Union, and the American Academy for the Advancement of Science, have arrived at the much the same conclusion.

There is a "global warming denial" industry in America.

Global warming skeptics make up a tiny minority, perhaps a dozen or so out of 2,500 scientists who specialize in the field.

Nevertheless, well-funded special interests led by the energy companies have invested considerable sums of money in a campaign aimed at convincing Americans and their elected officials that global warming is not a serious problem. Their motive is to block the passage of climate legislation that would hurt their bottom line. According to Ross Gelbspan: "Since the early 1990s, the fossil fuel lobby has mounted an extremely effective campaign of deception and disinformation designed to persuade policymakers, the press, and the public that the issue of climate change is stuck in scientific uncertainty."[11] Energy companies have contributed to research and advocacy organizations called "think tanks" and offered financial support to those scientists who still dispute the consensus about global warming.

Despite their low standing in the scientific community, skeptics have had an impact on policy makers. In 2003, James Inhofe of Oklahoma said on the floor of the U.S. Senate: "With all of the hysteria, all of the fear, all of the phony science, could it be that man-made global warming is the greatest hoax ever perpetrated on the American people? It sure sounds like it."[12] In that speech, Inhofe quoted from a scientific paper which concluded that the Earth was actually warmer during the Middle Ages than it is now—a claim that many scientists dispute. It turned out that four of the paper's five authors were affiliated with groups backed by the energy industry, and there was also a dispute as to whether their work even met the standards for inclusion in a scientific journal. Nevertheless, that paper was not only widely quoted but also influenced the nation's climate policy.

The nation's news media have also helped perpetuate the impression that scientists are divided over global warming. In an effort to avoid claims of bias, journalists tend to give equal weight to the consensus opinion and the critics, even though the facts weigh heavily against the critics' arguments. As a result, many Americans are still not sure whether humans are responsible for global warming. A survey taken in 2007 by the Pew Research Center for the People and the Press found that only 47 percent of Americans thought there was "solid evidence" that humans were responsible for global warming. Twenty percent blamed natural cycles, and another 16 percent thought there was no solid evidence of global warming.

Al Gore has accused the energy companies of using tactics similar to those used by the tobacco companies after scientists definitively linked cigarette smoking to cancer in the early 1960s. To illustrate his point, Gore quoted from a memo prepared by officials of the Brown and Williamson Tobacco Company: "Doubt is our product, since it is the best means of competing with the 'body of fact' that exists in the mind of the general public. It is also the means of establishing a controversy."[13]

Summary

The world's weather has gotten less predictable and more destructive, and there is growing evidence that global warming is responsible for it. Temperatures have risen in recent years and are probably higher now than at any time during the past thousand years. The warming has coincided with an increase in the concentration of carbon dioxide in the atmosphere to its highest level in hundreds of thousands of years, and that concentration is likely to increase further as the world's population and living standards continue to increase. In spite of wide agreement within the scientific community, powerful forces in this country continue to argue that humans are not to blame for global warming. Their efforts have confused Americans and so far blocked the passage of meaningful climate legislation.

Humans Are Not to Blame for Global Warming

In June 2001, three months after he announced that the United States would not sign the Kyoto Protocol, President George W. Bush discussed global warming. Regarding its causes, the president said:

> There is a natural greenhouse effect that contributes to warming. Greenhouse gases trap heat, and thus warm the earth because they prevent a significant proportion of infrared radiation from escaping into space. Concentration of greenhouse gases, especially CO_2, has increased substantially since the beginning of the industrial revolution. And the National Academy of Sciences indicates that the increase is due in large part to human activity.
>
> Yet, the Academy's report tells us that we do not know how much effect natural fluctuations in climate may have had on

45

warming. We do not know how much our climate could, or will change in the future. We do not know how fast change will occur, or even how some of our actions could impact it.[1]

Many Americans agree with President Bush that the scientific community rushed to judgment in blaming global warming on human-emitted greenhouse gases.

Natural cycles, not human activity, influence temperatures.

Critics of the Intergovernmental Panel on Climate Change (IPCC) dispute the notion that increased greenhouse gases concentration is the primary cause of higher temperatures. John Christy, a professor of atmospheric science at the University of Alabama–Huntsville and an IPCC member, argues: "Most of this warming occurred in the early part of the 20th century, before humans had boosted concentrations of greenhouse gases. . . . Sunspots, volcanic eruptions, El Niños, variations in aerosols, water vapor, carbon dioxide and methane from living creatures, and other unknown factors may all tweak the planet's temperature up and down."[2]

Christopher Horner, a senior fellow at the Competitive Enterprise Institute, adds that temperatures over the past 100 years did not move in the same direction as the amount of carbon dioxide in the air. Temperatures rose between 1895 and 1940, with the steepest warming trend between 1910 and 1935. That, however, was before humans burned significant amounts of fossil fuels. A cooling trend began after 1940 and bottomed out by the mid-1970s, at which time news stories discussed the possibility of "global cooling" and even a new ice age. This period of cooling, however, coincided with the period of greatest growth in fossil fuel consumption. Horner goes on to suggest that another force—namely, solar irradiance, or the amount of solar energy reaching the Earth—had a stronger influence on temperatures than greenhouse gases. The Sun, he points out, is a "variable star," meaning that the amount of solar irradiance reaching the Earth varies. Furthermore, it only takes a small change in solar irradiance—only about a few tenths of a percent—to affect temperatures on the Earth.

Horner points out that between 1975 and 1998, when temperatures rose, the Sun had become more active. On the other hand, episodes of solar "dimming" cooled the planet, often significantly:

> There is evidence that [the Sun] may have dimmed several times in the past 10,000 years, most conspicuously during the Little Ice Age that witnessed the demise of the Anasazi [a North American native people] and the Norsemen. Twice in the early fourteenth century, the Baltic Sea froze fast and glaciers came out of hibernation, grinding their way south to a point last reached 15,000 years earlier. Londoners roasted oxen on the Thames while the Flemish artist Pieter Brueghel, his fingers stiffened by the cold, kept up his spirits by painting peasants cavorting in the snow. At Plymouth Colony, a Pilgrim wrote of the 'cruell and fierce [winter] stormes' that racked the settlement; 200 years later iceboats plied the Hudson River almost as far south as New York City.[3]

S. Fred Singer and Dennis Avery, two leading critics of the greenhouse theory, argue that the so-called Modern Warming is the product of a recurring cycle of solar activity: "The Earth is warming but physical evidence from around the world tells us that human-emitted CO_2 (carbon dioxide) has played only a minor role in it. Instead, the mild warming seems to be part of a natural 1,500-year climate cycle (plus or minus 500 years) that goes back at least one million years."[4] They go on to say that the 1,500-year cycle is so powerful that it warmed the Earth even during ice ages, when trillions of tons of extra ice covered much of the Northern Hemisphere. The authors also believe that we are about 150 years into a warming cycle that, like all the others before it, will be followed by much cooler temperatures—regardless of how much carbon dioxide is in the atmosphere.

The Earth and its inhabitants are resilient.

Global warming skeptics maintain that a warming Earth will trigger natural forces that cool the planet. These negative feedbacks might have saved the planet in the distant past, when

Questioning the Link Between Human Activity and Global Warming

S. Fred Singer, a professor at George Mason University and a leading critic of global warming, and Dennis T. Avery, a fellow at the conservative Hudson Institute, recently wrote a book in which they argued that human-emitted greenhouse gases are not responsible for recent increases in the Earth's temperature. Singer and Avery believe that variations in the amount of solar energy reaching the Earth is the primary factor affecting temperatures and that solar energy—and temperatures—rise and fall over a 1,500-year-long cycle. They also believe that we are 150 years into a warming phase of the cycle.

In their book, the authors list eight arguments against the Intergovernmental Panel on Climate Change's finding that human activity—namely, burning fossil fuels that produce greenhouse gases—is causing global warming:

1. The Earth's 1,500-year climate cycle, not carbon dioxide concentrations, accounts for recent variation in the climate.
2. Much of the current warming happened by 1940, before most human-generated carbon dioxide was in the atmosphere.
3. Each added unit of carbon dioxide produces less warming than the unit before it.
4. "Official" temperature readings should be adjusted to reflect urban heat islands and changes in rural land use.
5. The Earth's surface temperatures have risen more than temperatures in the lower atmosphere, even though greenhouse theory states that carbon dioxide would warm the lower atmosphere first, after which the heat would radiate to the Earth's surface.

carbon dioxide concentrations rose to extreme levels. Patrick Michaels, a professor at the University of Virginia, explains:

> Some fossil records suggest the earth's carbon dioxide concentration in the geologic past was nearly *15 times* what it is today, and yet the temperature was less than 10°C (18°F) warmer than today. Contrary to current climate hype, this

6. Global warming produces more carbon dioxide, not the other way around.
7. Greenhouse theory predicts that carbon dioxide-driven warming would start and be strongest in the polar regions, but that is not happening.
8. There is a "heat vent" in the Earth's atmosphere over the Pacific Ocean. As temperatures rise, high clouds that trap heat dissipate, allowing the heat to escape.

Singer and Avery insist that the Earth's climate is the product of complex, long-term cycles that exert a much more powerful effect than higher concentrations of greenhouse gases. In addition to the 1,500-year climate cycle, they identify several longer-term cycles that cause variations in the amount of solar energy reaching the Earth.

- An elliptical cycle (100,000 years) in which the Earth's distance from the Sun changes as the shape of its orbit becomes more or less elliptical.

- An axial tilt cycle (41,000 years) in which the degree of tilt of the Earth's axis varies.

- A precession or "wobble" cycle (23,000 years) in the Earth's axis. This can lead to either extreme heat and cold or moderate temperatures.

The authors observe: "If all of this seems complicated, it is. (No wonder the simplistic Greenhouse Theory caught on with the public.) Climate forecasters must factor the 100,000-year elliptical cycle, the 41,000-year axial tilt cycle, and the 23,000-year precessions or 'wobble' cycle, plus the 1,500-year solar-driven cycle."

Source: S. Fred Singer and Dennis T. Avery, *Unstoppable Global Warming: Every 1,500 Years.* Lanham, Md.: Rowman & Littlefield Publishers, 2007.

planet therefore cannot undergo a "runaway" greenhouse effect from human emissions of carbon dioxide. We won't double carbon dioxide from its background value until late in this century (if we continue to intensively use fossil fuel, which is a dubious assumption for 100 years from now), and that's a far cry from a 15-fold increase.[5]

Scientists are starting to learn more about negative feedbacks. One theory, put forth by Richard Lindzen, a professor at the Massachusetts Institute of Technology, is the "iris effect." As temperatures rise, high clouds—which trap heat—dissipate, thus allowing excess heat to escape. Other scientists believe that low-level clouds are a negative feedback: Warmer oceans create more water vapor and ultimately, clouds that keep sunlight from entering the Earth's surface and warming it.

Not only is the Earth resilient, but so are the creatures that live on it. As a result, some individuals like S. Fred Singer and Dennis Avery take issue with the IPCC's prediction that higher temperatures will cause mass extinctions:

> Most of the world's animal species' "body types" were laid down during the Cambrian period, 600 million years ago, according to Jeffrey Levinton, chairman of the Department of Evolution and Ecology at the State University of New York–Stony Brook in a widely noted 1992 article in *Scientific American*. Thus we know that the major species have dealt successfully through the ages with new pest enemies, new diseases, ice ages, and global warmings higher than today's.[6]

They cite a number of reasons, ranging from hunting to asteroids colliding with the Earth, for die-offs that happened in the past. Furthermore, if animals can adapt to climate change, humans are even better able to do so. Thanks to technology such as air-conditioning, we cannot only survive but prosper in places with extreme temperatures.

Global warming skeptics also argue that the magnitude of the Modern Warming has been blown out of proportion. There have been times since the last ice age when the Earth was even warmer than it is today. During the Holocene Maximum, about 6,000 years ago, the Earth warmed to the point that much of eastern North America experienced drought so severe that sand dunes covered vast areas of the Great Plains. Furthermore, the Modern Warming only seems unusual because it follows centuries of cool temperatures. Christopher Horner argues: "Considering that it is only warm right now if you deliberately choose as your baseline a year colder than today, 'global warming' has been occurring since the six- to seven-hundred-year cooling period known as the Little Ice Age ended—to the tune of about one degree Fahrenheit in the past one-hundred-plus years. That's what all the fuss is about."[7]

Greenhouse theory is a scientific fad.

Even though human-caused global warming has been called a matter of scientific consensus, some scientists still disagree. To begin with, they argue that no scientific debate is ever closed. Galileo, for example, defied the scientific consensus of his day by insisting that the Earth revolved around the Sun, not the other way around. Some also argue that many of the facts about global warming are really opinions. John Christy explains:

> The science of climate deals with quantities we can measure in the natural world. Evidence for global warming, however, is often presented as the latest disaster-by-anecdote. And when characterizing the future, journalists employ these most useful words as their insurance policy—"seem," "if," "might," and "could"—before launching into a brutalizing description of the latest disaster and its potential for getting worse. (Anything *might* happen.) Rarely are *numbers*, which can be measured objectively, reported in such stories.[8]

(continues on page 54)

Senator Inhofe's Case Against Global Warming

James Inhofe, a U.S. senator from Oklahoma, is Congress's most outspoken critic of climate legislation. On July 28, 2003, on the floor of the Senate, Inhofe delivered a now-famous speech entitled "The Science of Climate Change." It was a wide-ranging attack on the Kyoto Protocol, the Intergovernmental Panel on Climate Change, and measures aimed at reducing greenhouse gas emissions. Here are some excerpts from that speech:

Much of the debate over global warming is predicated on fear, rather than science. Global warming alarmists see a future plagued by catastrophic flooding, war, terrorism, economic dislocations, droughts, crop failures, mosquito-borne diseases, and harsh weather—all caused by human-made greenhouse gas emissions....

Today, even saying there is scientific disagreement over global warming is itself controversial. But anyone who pays even cursory attention to the issue understands that scientists vigorously disagree over whether human activities are responsible for global warming, or whether those activities will precipitate natural disasters....

I would submit, furthermore, that not only is there a debate, but the debate is shifting away from those who subscribe to global warming alarmism. After studying the issue over the last several years, I believe that the balance of the evidence offers strong proof that natural variability is the overwhelming factor influencing climate....

I believe it is extremely important for the future of this country that the facts and the science get a fair hearing. Without proper knowledge and understanding, alarmists will scare the country into enacting its ultimate goal: making energy suppression, in the form of harmful mandatory restrictions on carbon dioxide and other greenhouse emissions, the official policy of the United States.

Such a policy would induce serious economic harm, especially for low-income and minority populations. Energy suppression, as official government and nonpartisan private analyses have amply confirmed, means higher prices for food, medical care, and electricity, as well as massive job losses and drastic reductions in gross domestic product, all the while providing virtually no environmental benefit. In other words: a raw deal for the American people and a crisis for the poor....

The [Kyoto Protocol] would have required the U.S. to reduce its emissions 31% below the level otherwise predicted for 2010. Put another way, the U.S. would have had to cut 552 million metric tons of CO_2 per year by 2008–2012. As the Business Roundtable pointed out, that target is "the equivalent of having to eliminate all current emissions from either the U.S. transportation sector, or the utilities sector (residential and commercial sources), or industry."...

Though such countries as China, India, Brazil, South Korea, and Mexico are signatories to Kyoto, they are not required to reduce their emissions, even though they emit nearly 30 percent of the world's greenhouse gases. And within a generation they will be the world's largest emitters of carbon, methane and other such greenhouse gases....

What gets obscured in the global warming debate is the fact that carbon dioxide is not a pollutant. It is necessary for life. Numerous studies have shown that global warming can actually be beneficial to mankind....

During the last few hundred thousand years, the earth has seen multiple and repeated periods of glaciation. Each of these "Ice Ages" has ended because of dramatic increases in global temperatures, which had nothing to do with fossil fuel emissions....

These cycles of warming and cooling have been so frequent and are often so much more dramatic than the tiny fractional degree changes measured over the last century that one has to wonder if the alarmists are simply ignorant of geological and meteorological history or simply ignore it to advance an agenda....

As it turns out, Kyoto's objective has nothing to do with saving the globe. In fact it is purely political. A case in point: French President Jacques Chirac said during a speech at The Hague in November of 2000 that Kyoto represents "the first component of an authentic global governance." So, I wonder: are the French going to be dictating U.S. policy? ...

So what have we learned from the scientists and economists I've talked about today?

1. The claim that global warming is caused by man-made emissions is simply untrue and not based on sound science.
2. CO_2 does not cause catastrophic disasters—actually it would be beneficial to our environment and our economy.

(continues)

(continued)
3. Kyoto would impose huge costs on Americans, especially the poor.
4. The motives for Kyoto are economic not environmental—that is, proponents favor handicapping the American economy through carbon taxes and more regulations.

With all of the hysteria, all of the fear, all of the phony science, could it be that man-made global warming is the greatest hoax ever perpetrated on the American people? It sure sounds like it.

Source: "The Science of Climate Change," Senate Floor Statement by U.S. Senator James Inhofe, Chairman, Committee on the Environment and Public Works, July 28, 2003.

(continued from page 51)

Scientists are not immune from bias, and some argue that the scientific community is predisposed to blame humans for global warming. Jens Bischof, a professor at Old Dominion University, observes that in science, as in other fields, research is often guided by an a priori idea, which could also be called a belief. He continues: "In the case of global warming, this belief is that, if enormous amounts of greenhouse gases are released into the atmosphere, a temperature rise must occur. This prior assumption has guided scientific thinking and triggered a true deluge of investigations, all desperately trying to prove just that. What has been totally forgotten is the fact that natural climate changes occur as well as manmade ones, and on time scales on the order of decades, in some cases."[9] Some even believe that the evidence will one day discredit the greenhouse theory and that scientists of the future will wonder why it ever gained such wide acceptance.

Critics also allege that human-caused global warming has become the "politically correct" position, meaning that scientists who question it risk reprisals. Canadian journalist Terence Cor-

coran describes how the scientific establishment tries to silence global warming dissenters:

> In short, under the new authoritarian science based on consensus, science doesn't matter much any more. If one scientist's 1,000-year chart showing rising global temperatures is based on bad data, it doesn't matter because we still otherwise have a consensus. If a polar bear expert says polar bears appear to be thriving, thus disproving a popular climate theory, the expert and his numbers are dismissed as being outside the consensus. If studies show solar fluctuations rather than carbon emissions may be causing climate change, these are damned as relics of the old scientific method. If ice caps are not all melting, with some even getting larger, the evidence is ridiculed and condemned. We have a consensus, and this contradictory science is just noise from the skeptical fringe.[10]

This kind of censorship is contrary to the very purpose of scientific inquiry—namely, testing existing beliefs using available facts—and raises questions as to the validity of the so-called consensus about global warming.

Climate activists have ulterior political motives.

Some think that climate activists are exploiting public fear about global warming and that their real objective is to advance a political agenda. Christopher Horner explains: "Spawned from the 1970s split of anti-modernists from the decades-old conservation movement, 'environmentalism' has matured into a nightmare for anyone who believes in private property, open markets, and limited government."[11] Many activists see environmental problems like global warming as proof that capitalism has failed, the Earth is overpopulated, and the way we live is destroying the

(continues on page 58)

FROM THE BENCH

Massachusetts v. EPA 549 U.S. 497 (2007)

In 1970, Congress passed the Clean Air Act, which directed the Environmental Protection Agency (EPA) to set national air quality standards to protect Americans against a list of pollutants, including carbon monoxide, sulfur dioxide, lead, and particulate soot. At the time, greenhouse gases were not a high priority. However, §202(a)(1) of the act (42 U.S.C. §7521(a)(1)) contained broad language directing the EPA to adopt rules covering "any air pollutant" from new motor vehicles that "cause, or contribute to, air pollution which may reasonably be anticipated."

In 1999, a group of 19 private organizations petitioned the EPA to regulate greenhouse gas emissions from new motor vehicles under §202 of the Clean Air Act. After a lengthy rule-making process, the EPA denied the petition. The agency gave two major reasons for doing so. First, it did not believe that the Clean Air Act authorized it to regulate greenhouse gases. Second, even if it could regulate greenhouse gases, doing so would be unwise because the evidence of human-induced global warming was still inconclusive; and even if it acted, its regulations might interfere with the Bush administration's global warming strategy, which included negotiations with foreign governments.

A group of states, cities, and advocacy groups filed a petition challenging the EPA's decision in the U.S. Court of Appeals for the District of Columbia Circuit. They argued that the EPA failed to carry out its duty under the Clean Air Act. The EPA moved to dismiss the petition on the grounds that the petitioners had no legal standing—in other words, they had no right to bring the matter to court because they could not link the EPA's greenhouse gas decision to any injuries they allegedly suffered. The case went to the U.S. Supreme Court, which, in *Massachusetts v. Environmental Protection Agency*, ordered the EPA to determine whether greenhouse gas emissions from vehicles were enough of a danger to justify regulatory action.

The vote was 5 to 4. Justice John Paul Stevens, who wrote the majority opinion, first concluded that the case was properly before the Court because the state of Massachusetts had legal standing. That was so because one effect of global warming, rising ocean levels, had already begun to affect that state's coastal land, and the EPA's failure to regulate greenhouse gases contributed to global warming. Stevens also noted that motor vehicles accounted for one-third of this country's carbon emissions and 6 percent of the worldwide total. He said, "While it may

be true that regulating motor-vehicle emissions will not by itself reverse global warming, it by no means follows that we lack jurisdiction to decide whether EPA has a duty to take steps to slow or reduce it."

Stevens next concluded that the EPA's decision was "arbitrary and capricious" because greenhouse gases fell within the Clean Air Act's broad and flexible definition of "air pollutant." Furthermore, even though Congress enacted climate-related legislation after it passed the Clean Air Act, Stevens found that those laws were not inconsistent with the EPA's duty under the Clean Air Act to regulate air pollutants. He added that the Energy Policy and Conservation Act, which directed the Transportation Department to set miles-per-gallon standards for vehicles, did not bar the EPA from setting greenhouse gas standards for those same vehicles.

Stevens next rejected the EPA's contention that it was unwise to regulate greenhouse gases at this time. He found that the Clean Air Act obligated the EPA to act unless it either determined that greenhouse gases did not contribute to global warming or provided a reasonable explanation why it could not act. In this case, none of the reasons offered by the agency justified its failure to determine whether greenhouse gases were in fact a danger.

There were two dissenting opinions. Chief Justice John Roberts argued that there was no "case and controversy" to be decided because the very nature of global warming made it impossible to blame any specific injuries—assuming they had occurred—on the EPA's inaction. He pointed out that global warming was a worldwide problem, the EPA regulated only a tiny fraction of the world's greenhouse gases, and sea levels might rise even if the EPA were to regulate greenhouse gases. Roberts observed that not hearing this case "involves no judgment on whether global warming exists, what causes it, or the extent of the problem" but would only amount to holding that global warming policy should be made by the elected branches of government, not the courts. Justice Antonin Scalia, who agreed with Roberts that the Court should not have heard this case, also maintained that the EPA had offered good reasons for concluding that it was unwise to regulate greenhouse gases. In addition, he contended that the Clean Air Act applied only to pollutants at or near ground level, not those found through-out the Earth's atmosphere.

In July 2008, the EPA responded to the Court's decision by asking for public comments on what, if anything, it should do about greenhouse gases. This was the first step in the agency's rule-making process.

(continued from page 55)
planet. Some would like to use global warming as an excuse for establishing a regulatory structure that dictates how we can use energy, in the name of "saving the human race." The end result will be a loss of both freedom and prosperity.

Climate activists tend to come from well-off industrialized nations and have little understanding of how the world's poorest people suffer because of lack of access to modern energy. Relying on assumptions rather than data, environmentalists too often refuse to consider alternative sources of energy, because they assume most alternatives are worse for the environment than burning fossil fuels. If, for argument's sake, human-made CO_2 *is* causing global warming, then their positions on issues aggravate the problem because they prevent energy alternatives from being used. For example, activists' opposition to nuclear power plants—which emit less carbon dioxide than coal- or gas-fired plants—illustrates their shortsightedness. They insisted that Kyoto's drafters not give emissions credits to developing countries that build new nuclear plants, even though 80 percent of France's electricity comes from such plants. James Lovelock, the British scientist who coined the controversial "Gaia principle" that envisions the Earth as a self-regulating organism, said: "I am a Green, and I entreat my friends in the movement to drop their wrongheaded objection to nuclear energy. Every year that we continue burning carbon makes it worse for our descendants. Only one immediately available source does not cause global warming, and that is nuclear energy."[12] In the United States as well, activists have brought the construction of new nuclear plants to a standstill. As a result, American utility companies had to meet this country's demand for energy by burning an extra 400 million tons (363 million metric tons) of coal a year. Had that coal not been burned, the United States could have met Kyoto's targets.

Finally, some critics believe that international organizations involved in climate policy are biased, especially against the United States. They also believe that Kyoto is the work of United Nations bureaucrats and climate activists and that the IPCC has injected politics into science. S. Fred Singer notes that just a fraction of the scientists who work on the IPCC's reports are allowed to approve their final version and after that, the reports are edited by a mere handful of individuals—some of whom are governmental officials, not scientists. Singer adds that the most widely quoted statement in the IPCC's 1995 *Summary for Policymakers*—that "the balance of evidence suggests there is a discernible human influence on global climate"—was added by nonscientists *after* the scientists had completed their work. He accuses the officials who inserted that language of a serious breach of scientific ethics.

Summary
Human-caused global warming is a "politically correct" position from which no dissent is allowed. The issue has been exploited by activists to promote their political and economic agenda. Despite claims of a consensus on global warming, some scientists insist that forces other than greenhouse gases cause global temperatures to change. Variations in the amount of solar energy have a stronger influence than greenhouse gases, and the current warming coincides with a period of more intense solar activity. In relative terms, the Modern Warming trend is modest; and besides, a warmer Earth poses little threat to humans, who are capable of adapting to it. In any event, higher temperatures will trigger negative feedback mechanisms and prevent unstoppable warming.

Global Warming Is a Serious Threat

I n his 2004 book *Boiling Point*, Ross Gelbspan listed some ominous signs that the Earth's climate was changing:

- The entire ecosystem of the North Sea was found to be in a state of collapse because of rising water temperatures.

- Europe experienced an extraordinary heat wave in the summer of 2003. What made it so deadly was higher nighttime temperatures resulting from the accumulation of greenhouse gases in the air.

- In September 2003, the biggest ice sheet in the Arctic, 150 square miles in area and 80 feet thick, collapsed from warming surface waters.

- That same month, scientists discovered that oceans were not only becoming more acidic but the acidity level had changed more in the past 100 years than in the 10,000 years before that.

- By the fall of that year, an 18-month drought in Australia had cut farm incomes in half and left many scientists wondering whether the continent would be in a state of permanent drought.

Climate activists warn that these phenomena are mild compared to those we could experience if global warming goes unchecked.

Global warming will grow worse in the future.

According to the Intergovernmental Panel on Climate Change (IPCC), the Earth's average temperature increased by about 1°F (0.6°C) during the last century. A further rise in temperatures is all but certain because the carbon dioxide resulting from past emissions will further affect our climate. Mayer Hillman, Tina Fawcett, and Sudhir Chella Rajan explain: "The delayed effects from the current warming have to reach a state of equilibrium as the extra energy distributes itself between atmosphere, oceans, and land. For this reason, global increases in mean surface temperatures, rising sea levels from thermal expansion of the oceans, and melting ice sheets are projected to continue for hundreds of years. So, even if all fossil fuel use ceased tomorrow, the climate would continue to change."[1]

James Hansen and his colleagues recently concluded that extra solar energy currently stored in the oceans will eventually warm the Earth by an additional 0.71°F to 1.25°F (0.4°C to 0.7°C).

The IPCC relies on climate models, which are highly sophisticated computer programs based on the laws of physics, to estimate the likely effects of greenhouse gas emissions. Depending on how fast world population rises and living standards improve, and how high emission levels rise in the future, the models' "best estimates" forecast a temperature increase between 3.2°F and 7.1°F (1.8°C and 4.0°C) by the end of the twenty-first century. Some believe that the IPCC's findings understate the severity of the global warming. Joseph Romm, a senior follow at the Center for American Progress, explains:

> Because the political leadership of every single member country—including Saudi Arabia, China and the United States—must agree to every word, the language in IPCC summaries tends to get watered down. Thus the IPCC reports are almost certainly understating both the pace and scale of climate change. In fact, the direct observational evidence makes clear that key climate change impacts—sea ice loss, ice sheet melting, sea level rise, temperature, and expansion of the tropics (a prelude to desertification)—all are either near the top or actually in excess of their values as predicted by the IPCC's climate models. The models are missing key amplifying feedbacks that have already begun to accelerate the rate of climate change.[2]

Global warming will make the Earth less habitable.

One serious consequence of global warming is higher ocean levels resulting from the melting of polar ice. There are indications that the sea ice over the Arctic Ocean is approaching irreversible decline. Peter Wadhams, an oceanographer at Cambridge University in England, warned that the ice could disappear entirely in the summer as early as 2020. Even worse consequences will occur if the massive ice sheet over Greenland disappears. A team of scientists recently concluded that this could happen in as little as 300 years and estimate that the result would be ocean levels more than 20 feet (6 meters, or m) deeper than they are now. Joseph Romm explains how serious a disaster this would be: "[M]any people seem to think scientists are warning about a one-time sea level rise, say a few feet, which would be painful, but still fairly straightforward to adapt to. In fact, we are potentially talking about sea level rise of 6 to 12 inches a decade by century's end, with that rate continuing for centuries. It's not at all clear how future generations would adapt to such an ongoing catastrophe."[3]

At the same time, global warming will cause much of the Earth to become drier. Higher temperatures will draw more moisture out of the soil, offsetting an expected increase in rainfall in many areas. Already, more than 1,300 square miles (336,698 hectares) of land around the world turn to desert every year, and that trend is accelerating. The United States, too, is vulnerable. A recent study predicted permanent drought by 2050 throughout the Southwest, where millions of Americans now live. Higher temperatures will trigger water shortages caused by the melting of glaciers, such as those in the Himalayan mountain system in Asia. The Himalayas contain 100 times as much ice as the Alps and provide more than half of the drinking water for 40 percent of the world's population. Fresh water is already running short in parts of China, India, and Africa. In this country, there are fears that the Colorado River and other sources of water cannot keep up with the Southwest's growing population and that global warming will make the expected water shortages even more serious.

Recently, the U.S. government's Climate Change Science Program released a report linking global warming to extreme weather such as the torrential rains that caused widespread flooding in the Midwest in 2008. Extreme weather is already a major killer. In 1998, flooding in Central America caused by Hurricane Mitch killed 11,000 people. Five years later, a heat wave swept Europe, killing 15,000 there. Jonathan Patz, a professor at Johns Hopkins University, observed: "Climatologists have

(continues on page 67)

How Global Warming Could Affect Us Later This Century

Part of the Intergovernmental Panel on Climate Change's *Fourth Assessment Report* dealt with warming-related impacts on the Earth. The panel warned that unless greenhouse gas emissions fall, the global climate system will probably experience larger changes during the twenty-first century than during the twentieth century. It also projected that the effects of global warming will, for the most part, be harmful.

The IPCC projected a number of regional-scale changes, including these:

- Greater warming over land and at the highest northern latitudes than for Earth as a whole.
- The loss of snow and ice cover, with Arctic late-summer sea ice disappearing almost entirely by the late twenty-first century.
- A very likely increase (better than 9 chances in 10) in the frequency of extreme heat, heat waves, and heavy precipitation.
- A likely increase (better than two chances in three) in the intensity of hurricanes, along with the movement of tropical storm tracks into nontropical latitudes.
- A very likely increase in precipitation at high latitudes and a likely decrease in precipitation in most subtropical land regions.

The panel also expressed high confidence (at least 80 percent certainty) that by the middle of the twenty-first century, annual river runoff and water availability will decrease in some dry regions in the mid-latitudes and tropics as well as high confidence that many semi-arid areas such as the Mediterranean basin, the western United States, southern Africa, and northeast Brazil will lose water.

The IPCC also projected the impact of global warming on specific regions of the world.

In Africa:

- By 2020, between 75 and 250 million people will be exposed to increased water stress; and in some countries, yields from rain-fed agriculture could fall by up to 50 percent, resulting in malnutrition and loss of food security.

- By 2080, the amount of semi-arid land will grow by 5 to 8 percent.
- Toward the end of the twenty-first century, higher sea levels will affect low-lying coastal areas with large populations, forcing some countries to spend 5 to 10 percent of their gross domestic product on defending against flooding.

In Asia:

- Coastal areas will face the greatest risk of flooding due to higher sea levels and greater river runoff.
- Sickness and death resulting from flood- and drought-related diarrhea will increase due to changes in rainfall patterns.
- By the 2050s, fresh water will become less available, especially in large river basins.

In Australia and New Zealand:

- By 2020, significant loss of biodiversity will occur in some ecologically rich sites, including the Great Barrier Reef and Queensland Wet Tropics.
- By 2030, water security problems will become worse and production from agriculture and forestry will decline in some areas due to increased drought and fire.
- By 2050, coastal development will increase the risks associated with higher sea levels and more severe and frequent storms.

In Europe:

- There will be a greater risk of inland flash floods, coastal flooding, and erosion due to storminess and higher sea levels.
- In the mountains, glaciers will retreat and snow cover will diminish.
- In some areas, as many as 60 percent of species will disappear.
- In southern Europe, temperatures will rise and drought will become more severe. As a result, hydropower potential and crop productivity will decrease and summer tourism will fall off.
- Health risks due to heat waves and wildfires will grow worse.

(continues)

(continued)

In Latin America:

- By mid-century, higher temperatures and less water in the soil will cause grassland to replace tropical forest in the eastern Amazon.
- Tropical areas will lose biodiversity as species become extinct.
- Crop and livestock production will decline, endangering food security in some areas and putting more people at risk of going hungry.
- Changing precipitation patterns and the disappearance of glaciers will reduce the amount of water available for human consumption, agriculture, and energy generation.

In North America:

- Western mountains will lose snowpack. There will be more winter flooding and less water flow in the summer, which will increase competition for scarce water resources.
- In the early twenty-first century, moderate warming will cause a 5 to 20 percent increase in agricultural yields; on the other hand, crops that are near the warm end of their suitable range or that depend on scarce water will face major challenges.
- Hot-weather cities will face an increased number of heat waves.
- Coastal areas will be increasingly stressed by the combined effects of global warming, development, and pollution.

In the polar regions:

- Glaciers will shrink and ice sheets will become thinner, threatening many creatures, including migratory birds and polar bears.
- There will be detrimental impacts on infrastructure and traditional indigenous ways of life.
- Ecosystems will become more vulnerable to invasive species.

On small islands:

- Higher sea levels will leave populations more vulnerable to storm surges.
- Eroding beaches and deteriorating coastlines will affect local resources.

- By mid-century, many small islands will not have enough water to meet their needs during the dry season.
- Islands, especially those in middle and high latitudes, will face an increased risk of invasive species.

Finally, the IPCC warned that even people who live far from the worst effects of global warming could still be at risk if they are poor, very young, or very old.

Source: United Nations Intergovernmental Panel on Climate Change, *Fourth Assessment Report. Climate Change 2007: Synthesis Report. Summary for Policymakers*. Geneva, Switzerland, 2007.

(continued from page 63)

long remarked that global warming will not simply manifest itself by a gradual climb in average temperatures. Rather, it is the frequency and intensity of extreme climatic events—such as heat waves, droughts, floods, and storms—that are expected to occur."[4] Future weather disasters also could lead to outbreaks of disease if large numbers of people are forced from their homes or lose electricity for an extended time.

Global warming will breed terrorism and conflict.

Over time, global warming will reduce the amount of habitable land. When crops fail and water runs out, conflict becomes much more likely. History tells us that when humans face starvation, they take what weapons they can find and invade more promising regions, often going to war with those who are already there. The conflict in Darfur in central Africa, which has killed an estimated 500,000 people, has been blamed on dwindling rainfall and cropland turning to desert as the Earth warms. A UN official remarked: "It illustrates and demonstrates what is increasingly becoming a global concern. . . . It doesn't take a genius to work out that as the desert moves southwards there is a physical limit to what [ecological] systems can sustain, and so you get one group displacing another."[5]

"Resource wars" will become a growing threat to world peace. Thomas Homer-Dixon, the director of the Trudeau Center for Peace and Conflict Studies at the University of Toronto, wrote: "Climate stress may well represent a challenge to international security just as dangerous—and more intractable—than the arms race between the United States and the Soviet Union during the cold war or the proliferation of nuclear weapons among rogue states today."[6] Homer-Dixon also noted that global warming-related conflicts could lead to guerrilla attacks, insurgencies, and terrorism. Ross Gelbspan raises the possibility that global warming could lead to another terrorist attack on the United States: "The continuing indifference by the United States to atmospheric warming . . . will almost guarantee more anti-U.S. attacks from people whose crops are destroyed by weather extremes, whose populations are afflicted by epidemics of infectious disease, and whose borders are overrun by environmental refugees."[7]

Global warming could become self-reinforcing.

In 2000, Peter Cox and his associates wrote an article in the British magazine *Nature* that warned about feedback mechanisms. Author Mark Lynas explains:

> Whilst previous models had treated rising temperatures as a simple linear process, Cox's team realised that land and ocean systems would not remain static during rapid global warming. They would *themselves* be affected by the changing climate. In the case of the oceans, warmer seas absorb less CO_2, leaving more of it to accumulate in the atmosphere and further intensify[ing] global warming. On land, matters would be even worse. Huge amounts of carbon are currently stored in the globe's soils, the half-rotted remains of

Many scientists believe that some of the most dramatic evidence of global warming is seen when large chunks of glaciers break off and collapse into the sea. Global warming skeptics, however, argue that the shrinking of glaciers is due to less precipitation and point out that glaciers were retreating during the mid-twentieth century when global temperatures were falling.

long-dead vegetation. . . . As soil warms, bacteria speed up their work to break down this stored carbon, releasing it back into the atmosphere as carbon dioxide.[8]

The Arctic sea ice is the most-discussed feedback mechanism. As the ice disappears, the surface of the Arctic Ocean will

Climate "Tipping Points"

In its latest assessment report, the Intergovernmental Panel on Climate Change (IPCC) warned that human-caused global warming could lead to abrupt or irreversible impacts, depending on how fast and by how much temperatures rise.

Recently, a team led by Timothy Lenton of the University of East Anglia in England set out to identify those parts of the Earth that are at greatest risk of irreversible climate change. Lenton offered a formal definition of "tipping element": a subsystem of the Earth that is at least subcontinental in scale and that can be switched—under certain circumstances—into a qualitatively different state by small disturbances.

Lenton's team reviewed the literature on climate change and conducted a workshop that brought together 36 leading experts to draw up a "short list" of tipping elements that deserve the attention of policy makers. They then asked a group of experts to rank the tipping elements according to their sensitivity to global warming and the uncertainty surrounding them. In February 2008, they reported their findings in the *Proceedings of the National Academy of Sciences*. Nine tipping elements made Lenton's team's short list:

- The melting of Arctic sea ice

- The collapse of the Greenland ice sheet

- The collapse of the West Antarctic ice sheet

- A shutoff of the Atlantic conveyor (the Gulf Stream is the best-known element of this system)

- More persistent or frequent El Niño conditions

change from light to dark, causing the ocean to absorb heat instead of reflecting it. That, in turn, will raise global temperatures further, causing ice elsewhere in the Arctic to begin melting. There are other potential feedback mechanisms as well. One is the loss of forests, which act as "carbon sinks"—that is, they absorb and store carbon dioxide. Cutting down forests is the

- Changes to the Indian summer monsoon
- Changes to the Sahara/Sahel and West African monsoon
- Dying of the Amazon rain forest
- Dying of the boreal forests (those found in northern latitudes)

The experts called the melting of the Arctic sea ice "the greatest and clearest threat" because the ice will go into irreversible decline once temperatures rise to between 0.89°F and 3.6°F (0.5°C and 2.0°C) above those at the beginning of the twentieth century—a point that already might have been reached. They also expressed serious concern over the melting of the Greenland ice sheet, which stood a 50 percent chance of melting unstoppably. Although it would likely take at least 300 years for the ice sheet to melt, its doing so would raise global sea levels by more than 20 feet (6 m).

Lenton's team also noted that there was substantial uncertainty as to whether the tropics, the boreal zone, or west Antarctica would pass a tipping point. Nevertheless, those regions are sensitive enough that they might surprise the world by doing so, perhaps later this century. As for the collapse of the Atlantic conveyor, "the archetypal example of a tipping element," the team called that "a less immediate threat" but cautioned that the conveyor's long-term fate under significant warming "remains a source of concern."

The team concluded: "Given the large uncertainty that remains about tipping elements, there is an urgent need to improve our understanding of the underlying physical mechanisms determining their behavior, so that policy makers are able 'to avoid the unmanageable, and to manage the unavoidable.'"

Source: Timothy M. Lenton et al., "Tipping Elements in the Earth's Climate System," *Proceedings of the National Academy of Science*, February 12, 2008, pp. 1786–93.

equivalent of increasing emissions. (Forest fires will also occur more frequently as temperatures rise and timber becomes drier; these fires will dump even more carbon dioxide into the atmosphere.) Another feedback mechanism is the growing acidity of the oceans as carbon dioxide accumulates in them. As the oceans grow more acidic, the water kills off sea creatures that absorb carbon dioxide, leaving even more unabsorbed carbon dioxide in the atmosphere. Still another feedback mechanism is the diminishing ability of plants and soil to absorb carbon dioxide as the Earth warms; as that happens, more of the gas stays in the atmosphere. There is evidence that the Earth's carbon sinks are weakening, and scientists are concerned about it. In 2007, a group of British researchers found that since the twenty-first century began, carbon dioxide concentrations grew 35 percent faster than expected. The study's author, Corinne Le Quere, called the results a shock and said: "We expected that emissions would grow because of the expansion in the world economy but not because of a weakening in the sinks. Only the most extreme climate models predicted this. We didn't think it would happen until the second half of the century."[9]

We face the threat of runaway global warming.

In 2007, the IPCC warned: "Anthropogenic warming could lead to some impacts that are abrupt or irreversible, depending upon the rate and magnitude of the climate change."[10] The panel did not say how much or how fast temperatures had to rise in order for that to happen, leaving policy makers and scientists to try to define maximum "safe" levels. In 1996, the European Union's environment ministers recommended that global average temperatures not rise by more than 3.6°F (2°C) above pre-industrial levels and that the atmosphere's carbon dioxide concentration should not go above 550 parts per million (ppm)—about twice the pre-Industrial Revolution level. However, a growing number of scientists believe that those levels are dangerously high. James Hansen argues that the current carbon dioxide concentration,

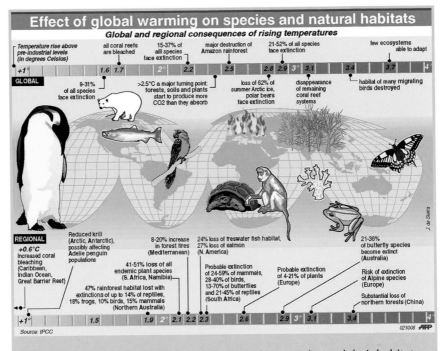

Effect of global warming on species and natural habitats
Global and regional consequences of rising temperatures

Above, the impact of global warming on various species and their habitats is illustrated. Many scientists are concerned that global warming may lead to worldwide extinctions, possibly as many as a million species lost by 2050.

385 ppm, is already causing damage to the planet and warns that irreversible consequences will occur if levels stay at or above this level for a sustained period of time.

A team of scientists led by Professor Timothy Lenton of the University of East Anglia in England explored possible "tipping elements," relatively small disturbances that "switch" much of the Earth into a qualitatively different state. Lenton's team concluded that "a variety of tipping elements could reach their critical point within this century under anthropogenic climate change. The greatest threats are tipping the Arctic sea-ice and the Greenland ice sheet, and at least five other elements could surprise us by

(continues on page 76)

If Global Temperatures Rose Six Degrees, What Would Happen?

Climate models, cited in Intergovernmental Panel on Climate Change (IPCC) *Third Assessment Report*, projected that global temperatures could rise by as much as 10.4°F (5.8°C) by the end of the twenty-first century. To find out what would happen if the world warmed by that much, journalist Mark Lynas read thousands of scientific papers dealing with how climate change affected life on Earth in the past. The result of his work was a book entitled *Six Degrees*.

An increase of *one degree* would bring about conditions like those of the Holocene Maximum, about 6,000 years ago. Then, much of the United States experienced drought worse than the Dust Bowl of the 1930s. Arctic ice would melt, giving way to ocean water, which will absorb more heat than ice and lead to further warming. Species could die out in sensitive areas such as the rain forests of northeast Australia. Low-lying island nations would be threatened by rising sea levels.

An increase of *two degrees* would cause severe droughts and water shortages in China's interior. As carbon dioxide accumulates, the Earth's oceans would become more acidic and less able to support life. As sea creatures that absorb carbon dioxide die off, more carbon dioxide stays in the atmosphere. Europe would suffer frequent heat waves as severe as the deadly one in 2003, which was called a "once-in-a-thousand-years" event. Because temperatures rise faster at higher altitudes, mountain glaciers would continue to shrink and Greenland's ice sheet would start to disappear. A two-degree rise could put hundreds of thousands of plant and animal species at risk of extinction.

An increase of *three degrees* would breed "super hurricanes" more powerful than anything humans have experienced so far. El Niño, and the extreme weather that it brings, could become a near-permanent occurrence. Higher temperatures would bring drought to southern Africa, forcing those who live there to flee—and fight for survival against neighbors who refuse to take them in. Asia's monsoons would become more intense but less predictable. At the same time, higher temperatures would melt Asia's massive glaciers, depriving large parts of the continent the water needed to grow crops and generate electric power. More and more crops would reach their "thermal tolerance threshold," beyond which they cannot grow. As the soil warms, bacteria will break down the huge amounts of carbon stored inside, returning it to the atmosphere as carbon dioxide. Rain forests in the Amazon basin would give way to grassland, perhaps as the result of a gigantic wildfire, and perhaps turn into a Sahara-type desert.

If temperatures rise by *four degrees*, the Arctic Ocean would become ice-free for the first time in several million years. The West Antarctic ice sheet could collapse into the ocean, raising ocean levels by 15 feet (4.6 m) or more. Coastal areas such as greater New York would flood, and the millions who live there would be forced inland. Land where crops can be grown would become scarcer, and mass starvation would be difficult to avoid. Higher temperatures would melt the permafrost in Siberia, Alaska, and northern Canada, releasing hundreds of billions of tons of greenhouse gases that had been trapped inside by below-freezing temperatures for millions of years. Southern Europe could become so hot that those who live there would be turned into climate refugees.

An increase of *five degrees* would empty most of the planet's underground reservoirs of water, making it more difficult yet to grow crops. Competition for the world's remaining arable land could lead China to invade Russia and the United States to invade Canada. Increasingly, humans would be concentrated toward the poles, and the Earth's population could fall to one billion or less. Conditions could resemble those of about 55 million years ago, when carbon dioxide levels topped 1,000 parts per million, oceans were acidic, and there were extremes of wet and dry. During that time, a massive die-off of sea creatures occurred. Scientists believe the die-off might have been the result of a huge eruption of a combination of methane and water loosened from the ocean depths. Even today, vast amounts of this substance remain trapped on the continental shelves underneath the oceans.

Left unchecked, global warming could lead to conditions similar to those of the end of the Permian period, about 250 million years ago. Then, a cataclysmic event wiped out nearly all life on Earth. Scientists are unsure what caused it, but one possibility is a greenhouse event that raised global temperatures by *six degrees*. Oceans were almost inhospitable to life, ferocious hurricanes raged, and erupting volcanoes released large quantities of carbon into the atmosphere. At plus-six degrees humans, too, are at risk of extinction. Lynas raised the possibility of "the ultimate nightmare scenario," super-eruptions of underwater methane that would be 10,000 times as powerful as all of the world's nuclear weapons combined.

Source: Mark Lynas, *Six Degrees: Our Future on a Hotter Planet*. London: Fourth Estate, 2007.

(continued from page 73)
exhibiting a nearby tipping point."[11] Another team of scientists, led by James Hansen, expressed similar concern over the irreversible loss of Arctic ice:

> If we stay our present course, using fossil fuels to feed a growing appetite for energy-intensive life styles, we will soon leave the climate of the Holocene, the world of prior human history. The eventual response to doubling pre-industrial atmospheric CO_2 likely would be a nearly ice-free planet. . . . Ocean and ice sheet inertias provide a buffer delaying full response by centuries, but there is a danger that human-made forcings could drive the climate system beyond tipping points such that change proceeds out of our control.[12]

Mark Lynas, who has read much of the scientific literature, suggests that global warming might become unstoppable once temperatures rise to 7.1°F (4°C) above pre-industrial levels. At that point, vast amounts of greenhouse gases under the frozen soil of the Arctic will escape into the atmosphere, causing even more warming. The end result of runaway global warming is a frightening prospect. Lynas believes that higher water temperatures could release methane gas currently trapped on the ocean floor. The highly combustible gas could become a massive fireball that would be far more devastating than the most powerful nuclear bomb. Al Gore described another possible dire outcome in a column in the *New York Times*:

> Consider this tale of two planets. Earth and Venus are almost exactly the same size, and have almost exactly the same amount of carbon. The difference is that most of the carbon on Earth is in the ground—having been deposited there by various forms of life over the last 600 million years—and most of the carbon on Venus is in the atmosphere.

As a result, while the average temperature on Earth is a pleasant 59 degrees, the average temperature on Venus is 867 degrees.[13]

Summary

The warming of the past century is mild compared to what could happen in the future. Additional warming is already "locked in" because of the actions of the greenhouse gases we have already emitted into the atmosphere. Temperatures will rise still more if we continue to emit at or above current levels. Higher temperatures are expected to cause flooding, drought, and more frequent episodes of extreme weather. Global warming will make the Earth a more hostile place for human beings, who will begin to fight one another for dwindling land and resources. Warming will trigger feedback mechanisms—natural forces that release more greenhouse gases into the atmosphere—and cause still more warming. The first feedback mechanism, the melting of the ice in the polar regions, is already occurring. At some point, global warming could become unstoppable.

The Dangers of Global Warming Are Exaggerated

T he Competitive Enterprise Institute's Christopher Horner argues that a range of factors influence the Earth's climate:

> The climate is always changing. Different parts of the planet are always getting colder or warmer, wetter or drier. Many things can cause this climate change. The sun has cycles, sometimes producing more energy, and sometimes producing less. The Earth's wobble and eccentric orbit mean that different parts of the planet will be exposed to varying amounts of heat over different periods. If more snow or land is exposed, more heat might be reflected. If more water is exposed, more heat will be absorbed. If the sky gets darkened by dust—caused by a volcano, a meteor, or pollution—it can make the planet colder. Land-use changes, Manmade or

otherwise, greatly impact local climate. Finally, there is the most famous (but still only one of many) factor in temperature: greenhouse gases.[1]

Horner and other critics of the greenhouse theory insist that the Intergovernmental Panel on Climate Change (IPCC) acted too hastily in blaming human-produced greenhouse gas emissions for the recent rise in global temperatures.

We do not fully understand climate.

The Earth's climate is a system with many variables, something that climate scientists themselves acknowledge. According to the American Association of State Climatologists (AASC): "Climate prediction is complex, with many uncertainties. The AASC recognizes climate prediction is an extremely difficult undertaking. For time scales of a decade or more, understanding the empirical accuracy of such prediction—called 'verification'—is simply impossible, since we have to wait a decade or more to assess the accuracy of the forecasts."[2] Thus it is an oversimplification to blame the recent warming on greenhouse gases alone.

Critics contend that the climate models that appeared in the IPCC's two latest assessment reports are not reliable forecasting tools. One of them, Freeman Dyson, a professor at Princeton University, remarked:

> [T]he climate models on which so much effort is expended are unreliable because they still use fudge-factors rather than physics to represent important things like evaporation and convection, clouds and rainfall. Besides the general prevalence of fudge-factors, the latest and biggest climate models have other defects that make them unreliable. With one exception, they did not predict the existence of El Niño. Since El Niño is a major feature of the observed climate, any model that fails to predict it is clearly deficient.[3]

Other critics add that models must account for so many variables that a small error in one part of a model can result in a highly inaccurate final answer.

Global warming is wrongly blamed for extreme weather.

Phenomena blamed on global warming happened long before carbon dioxide concentrations reached their present levels. For example, Al Gore warns that global warming will raise ocean levels, forcing millions of people to flee to higher ground. However, S. Fred Singer and Dennis Avery point out that sea levels have been rising naturally for some 6,000 years, and by a mere 2 inches

California's Proposed Greenhouse Gas Regulations for Vehicles

In 2002, California lawmakers passed the Pavley bill (Chapter 200, Statutes of 2002), which directed that state's Air Resources Board to set standards for emissions of carbon dioxide, methane, nitrous oxide, and hydrofluorocarbons—the primary pollutants that create global warming—from automobiles. Later, the board adopted rules that would require automakers to reduce emissions of those substances by 30 percent over 10 years.

The federal Clean Air Act of 1970 authorizes California to adopt environmental standards for vehicles that are stricter than federal requirements if it receives a waiver from the Environmental Protection Agency (EPA). If the EPA grants California's waiver request, other states are permitted to adopt California's stricter standards. Over the years, the EPA has granted California about 50 waivers covering anti-pollution measures such as catalytic converters, exhaust emission standards, and restrictions on leaded gasoline.

In December 2005, California applied to the EPA for a waiver to implement its motor vehicle global warming regulations. Two years later, the EPA administrator denied California's request. California then filed a petition with the U.S. Court of Appeals for the Ninth Circuit, challenging the EPA's denial (*California v.*

(5 centimeters) per century. Activists also warn that global warming will cause droughts. John Christy, a professor at the University of Alabama–Huntsville, responds: "Our country has experienced multidecadal droughts that completely overwhelm the effect of the 1930's experience [the Dust Bowl]. The five most significant droughts in the past 2,000 years all occurred prior to 1600. The Sand Hills of Nebraska, now covered with a layer of prairie foliage, were literally desert sand dunes during such droughts. This tells us that our nation should be aware that significant disruption is possible due to the natural variations of climate."[4]

Another claim of climate activists is that global warming will cause tropical diseases such as malaria to spread to cooler

Environmental Protection Agency, No. 08–70001 [U.S. Ct. App., 9th Cir., filed Jan. 2, 2008]), and 17 states have asked to join California's challenge.

In the meantime, the auto industry has filed suit to stop the regulations from taking effect if California receives an EPA waiver in the future. They argue that the regulations conflict with both federal law and the nation's foreign policy. However, in *Central Valley Chrysler-Jeep, Inc. v. Goldstene*, 529 F. Supp.2d 1151 (E.D. Cal. 2007), a federal court in California sided with the state. Judge Anthony Ishii concluded that the Clean Air Act gave equal authority to the federal government and California to regulate greenhouse gases, California's regulations did not conflict with the miles-per-gallon standards laid down by the Energy Policy and Conservation Act, and the regulations did not conflict with the nation's foreign policy.

Earlier that year, a federal court in Vermont heard a similar challenge to Vermont's proposed adoption of California's emissions regulations. In *Green Mountain Chrysler-Plymouth, Inc. v. Crombie*, 508 F. Supp. 2d 295 (D. Vt. 2007), Judge William Sessions III ruled for the state. He concluded that California's emission standards did not necessarily conflict with federal fuel economy standards, even though they might have an effect on fuel economy. Sessions also ruled that the automakers had not proved that the proposed regulations were technologically or economically infeasible or that they would adversely affect consumer choice or safety.

regions. However, malaria is not "tropical" (the worst recorded outbreak occurred in the Soviet Union during the 1920s), and better public health measures, not cooler temperatures, largely eradicated the disease from the developed world.

After Hurricane Katrina struck the Gulf Coast in 2005, activists quickly blamed the storm, as well as that year's record tropical activity, on global warming. Singer and Avery dispute the link between higher temperatures and greater frequency of such storms. They cite records kept by the British Royal Navy, which showed that major hurricanes made landfall in the Caribbean more often between 1701 and 1850, when temperatures and carbon dioxide concentrations were lower, than they did in the late twentieth century. In fact, an American Meteorological Society panel of experts said a year after Katrina: "First, no connection has been established between greenhouse gas emissions and the observed behavior of hurricanes. . . . Second, . . . a scientific consensus exists that any future changes in hurricane intensities will likely be small and in the context of observed natural variability."[5] The meteorologists went on to state that blaming hurricanes on global warming could invite criticism of legitimate climate research.

Finally, there are indications that the current warming trend is easing. A recent editorial in the *Wall Street Journal* said: "In the 1990s, virtually all climate models predicted warming from 2000–2010, but the new data confirm that so far there has been no warming trend in this decade for the U.S. Whoops. These simulation models are the basis for many of the forecasts of catastrophic warming by the end of the century that Al Gore and the media repeat time and again. We may soon be basing multitrillion dollar policy decisions on computer models whose accuracy we already know to be less than stellar."[6]

Activists exaggerate the seriousness of global warming.

Al Gore's 2006 book *An Inconvenient Truth* is full of dire predictions about what unchecked global warming could do to the planet. Gore is the latest in a series of authors who warned of environmental catastrophes that never materialized. In *Silent Spring* (1962), Rachel Carson foresaw an extinction of wildlife resulting from our use of pesticides. In *The Population Bomb* (1968), Paul Ehrlich concluded that overpopulation would soon trigger famine and mass starvation. The authors of *Limits to Growth* (1972) warned of the depletion of natural resources and predicted that the world's oil supply would run out in 20 years. The Competitive Enterprise Institute observes: "Not a single major prediction of ideological environmentalism has come true—no global famines, no cancer epidemics, and no resource depletion crisis."[7]

The media, too, have exaggerated the consequences of global warming. Many news stories about climate mention the plight of the polar bear: Global warming is shrinking its Arctic habitat, putting it in danger of becoming extinct. Bjorn Lomborg argues that polar bears are not facing extinction and adds that hunters, not global warming, are the number one threat to the bears. Media reports also point to the shrinking glaciers on Mount Kilimanjaro in Africa as evidence of dangerous global warming. However, S. Fred Singer and Dennis Avery blame the glaciers' disappearance on less precipitation and note that the glaciers were retreating during the mid-twentieth century when global temperatures were falling. Critics also point out that the media have a history of not only overdramatizing climate change but being wrong about it. During the 1970s, there was widespread concern that an ice age was about to begin. Lomborg notes how *Science Digest* pointed out in 1973:

> [A]t this point, the world's climatologists are agreed on only two things: that we do not have the comfortable distance of tens of thousands of years to prepare for the next ice age, and that how carefully we monitor our atmospheric pollution will have direct bearing on the arrival and nature of this weather crisis. The sooner man confronts these facts, these scientists say, the safer he'll be. Once the freeze starts, it will be too late.[8]

Even the IPCC is not above exaggerating the consequences of global warming. In 2001, the panel estimated that temperatures could rise by as much as 10.4°F (5.8°C) by the end of this century. Patrick Michaels, a professor at the University of

Nuisance Suits Against Emitters: An Ancient Theory Meets a Modern Problem

In their fight against global warming, California and a number of other states turned to the centuries-old legal theory of "public nuisance," under which the government can go to court to stop activity that unreasonably interferes with rights enjoyed by the public or that endangers life, health, or property. Pollution has traditionally fallen within the class of public nuisance. In their lawsuits, the states argued that nuisance theory also applied to carbon dioxide, which has been identified as the chief contributor to global warming. The states targeted the two industries that are the biggest emitters of carbon dioxide: automakers and electric utilities.

The first suit was the "power plant case," *State of Connecticut v. American Electric Power Company*, 406 F. Supp. 2d 265 (S.D.N.Y. 2005). Eight states, New York City, and several environmental groups, sued the American Electric Power Company and four other utility companies. The plaintiffs alleged that the companies were the nation's largest emitters of carbon dioxide, accounting for one-quarter of the industry's total emissions, or about 650 million tons (589 million metric tons) a year. They asked the court to declare the emissions a public nuisance, cap future emissions, and reduce the cap over at least a 10-year period. The utility companies asked the court to dismiss the case. Their main argument was that whether and how to limit greenhouse gases was a political question, one that should be decided by the president and Congress, not the courts.

Judge Loretta Preska granted the defendants' motion. In deciding whether the case raised a political question, she looked to six criteria laid down by the U.S. Supreme Court. The criterion most relevant to this case was whether a court could reach a decision without making the kind of "initial policy determination" that clearly belonged to the elected branches of government. In this case, the states were asking her to determine what was an appropriate level of emissions on the part of utility companies, and to do so against the backdrop of both

Virginia, remarks that "it is much more likely that future global warming would fall nearer the low end of the IPCC range, 1.4°C, rather than the high end. The IPCC has known that all along, yet they've let a hysterical environmental and popular press

---

the administration's negotiations with other countries about climate and the national-security implications of having enough electricity. Preska also found that Congress had not regulated carbon dioxide emissions, even though lawmakers had recognized the link between those emissions and global warming, and that global warming was a potentially serious problem. She added that the Environmental Protection Agency, which is in charge of enforcing federal environmental laws, had also decided against regulating emissions, in large part because it did not want to interfere with the president's climate policy.

The second case to be heard was the "auto case," *People of the State of California v. General Motors Corporation*, No. C06–057555 MJJ (U.S. Dist. Ct., N.D. Cal., September 17, 2007), in which California sued six of the world's largest automakers. The state alleged that the companies' products emitted about 300 million tons (272 million metric tons) of carbon dioxide and that automobiles were responsible for more than 30 percent of California's carbon dioxide emissions. Instead of a court order limiting emissions, California asked for damages to compensate its residents for the effects of global warming.

The auto companies moved to dismiss the lawsuit because it raised a political question. Judge Martin Jenkins agreed. His opinion incorporated much of Preska's reasoning from the power plant case. He added that it would be both premature and inappropriate for the courts to make climate-related decisions before the elected branches of government had done so, especially at a time when the administration was trying to persuade countries like China and India to cut their emissions. In Jenkins's view, it made no difference that California was asking for money damages instead of court-ordered emissions limits because the lawsuit still required him to decide what was a reasonable level of emissions and how much in damages Californians had suffered as the result of those emissions. That determination was further complicated by the fact that natural variations in climate also contribute to global warming, there was no way of tracing emissions gases to a specific source, and California had not explained how the automakers caused global warming-related injury to its residents.

run with apocalyptic scenarios touting the huge 5.8°C (10.4°F) warming."[9]

We face other, more serious problems.

Despite activists' claims, global warming is not the most serious problem humans face. Bjorn Lomborg explains: "[I]t is obvious that there are many other and more pressing issues for the third world, such as almost four million people dying from malnutrition, three million from HIV/AIDS, 2.5 million from indoor and outdoor air pollution, more than two million from lack of micronutrients (iron, zinc, and vitamin A), and almost two million from lack of clean drinking water."[10]

Poverty, not climate, is responsible for most threats to public health, and limits on greenhouse gases will neither eliminate those threats nor lead to higher living standards that will make people healthier. Thomas Gale Moore, a senior fellow at the Hoover Institution, notes that Singapore, a prosperous Asian city-state located close to the equator, is free of malaria, but the poorer rural areas of Malaysia, just a few hundred miles away, still suffer from it.

Furthermore, global warming poses no *immediate* threat. Even if temperatures rise substantially, most of the effects will not occur for decades. Therefore, instead of rushing to make large cuts in greenhouse gas emissions, it would be wiser to wait until scientists have a better idea of how global warming affects us and societies have more resources to fight it. Some believe that it is better policy to adapt to the effects of global warming when they come than act now to stop global warming itself. Hurricanes are prime candidates for adaptation. Lomborg notes that today's hurricanes are highly destructive because government fails to plan for them, not because they are more powerful than hurricanes of the past. He contends, "in a world with increasing hurricane damage from both global warming and societal factors, Kyoto could probably reduce the total increased damage by 0.5 percent, when simple preventative measures could reduce that same damage by about 50 percent—one hundred times better."[11]

Finally, some believe that the biggest climatic disaster we face is not warmer temperatures but the return of the glaciers. S. Fred Singer and Dennis Avery explain: "When it [the next ice age] comes, temperatures may plummet 15 degrees Celsius, with the high latitudes getting up to 40 degrees colder. Humanity and food production will be forced closer to the equator, as huge ice sheets expand in Canada, Scandinavia, Russia, and Argentina. Even Ohio and Indiana may gradually be encased in mile-thick ice, while California and the Great Plains could suffer century-long drought."[12]

The Earth has experienced ice ages in years past, and at regular intervals. Many believe that it is only a matter of time before the next one arrives.

A warmer earth is beneficial to humans.

Humans have not fared well during times of extreme cold. Seventy thousand years ago, the Earth experienced a "volcanic winter" followed by a thousand-year ice age. According to scientists at Stanford University, the human population might have dropped to 2,000, pushing our species to the brink of extinction. During the most recent ice age, it was much more difficult for humans to survive than it was during the interglacial period that followed. Even today, cold is deadlier to humans than heat. Europeans were shocked by the 2003 heat wave that killed 15,000 people, but Bjorn Lomborg points out that 1.5 million Europeans die from excess cold every year.

By contrast, humans prospered during previous warm periods. John Carlisle, the director of the Environmental Policy Task Force, discusses a warming trend that occurred during ancient times:

Between 6500 and 3500 B.C., the temperature increased from 58°F to 62°F. This is the warmest the Earth has been during the Holocene, which is why scientists refer to the period as the Holocene Maximum. Since the temperature of the Holocene Maximum is close to what global warming models project for the Earth by 2100, how Mankind faired during the era is instructive. The most striking fact is that it was during this period that the Agricultural Revolution began in the Middle East, laying the foundation for civilization.[13]

Between about 1000 and 1300 A.D., the Earth experienced a milder version of the Holocene Maximum. Carlisle explains: "The warming that occurred between 1000 and 1350 caused the ice in the North Atlantic to retreat and permitted Norsemen to colonize Iceland and Greenland. Back then, Greenland was actually green. Europe emerged from the Dark Ages in a period that was characterized by bountiful harvests and great economic prosperity. So mild was the climate that wine grapes were grown in England and Nova Scotia."[14] During that period, many of Europe's famous castles and cathedrals were built, suggesting that there were good crops, ample food supplies, and enough people who could work on major construction projects rather than on farms.

On the other hand, life was much harsher during the Little Ice Age that followed. The Viking settlers in Greenland died off. Glaciers advanced in Switzerland and Scandinavia, forcing villagers to flee to lower ground. Rivers in London and in St. Petersburg, Russia, froze over, as did the canals of The Netherlands. There were serious crop failures, famines, and disease due to the cooler climate. Colder weather was also accompanied by stronger storms, more floods and droughts, and more serious famines— the very phenomena that the IPCC warns will result from higher global temperatures. In fact, extreme weather occurred more often during colder periods than warmer ones.

Summary

The Earth's climate is highly complex, and even experts admit they do not fully understand it. The evidence of global warming is still uncertain, and in some cases unreliable. Climate models, in particular, are capable of producing large errors. The news media exaggerate the seriousness of global warming, and climate activists unfairly blame it for a variety of extreme weather. Over-dramatization of global warming has led policy makers to give it a higher priority than more serious and immediate problems such as disease and poverty. The unwise decisions we are making could, in the long run, reduce our ability to combat global warming. In any event, a warmer Earth is likely more beneficial to humans, and our main concern should be extreme cold, including a possible new ice age.

Governments, Including Ours, Must Take Action

Author and journalist Vijay Vaitheeswaran posed the following hypothetical question regarding global warming:

> What would a leader like Winston Churchill have done about climate change? Imagine that he had been presented with an emerging problem that could, if neglected, turn into a global disaster. Imagine that a response might require concerted global action and perhaps even economic sacrifice on the home front. Now imagine that his aides could not provide him with irrefutable evidence of that impending crisis. Would he have done nothing—or would he have started taking sensible precautions despite the uncertainty?[1]

Churchill, the famous British prime minister, mobilized his people to fight Nazi Germany during World War II. Climate activists insist that global warming is a threat as serious as an enemy invasion and that we need leaders like Churchill to come forward and mobilize the world for the fight against it.

Market forces alone cannot reduce emissions.

Some economists call global warming the greatest example of market failure the world has ever seen. In their opinion, the number one cause of that failure is government officials' failure to put a "price tag" on greenhouse gas emissions. Thus emitters have an incentive to treat the atmosphere as a vast dumping ground because no one will force them to pay for the environmental damage they do. Author Paul Roberts adds: "Though cheap, plentiful fossil fuels have clearly been key to our industrial success and continued economic vitality, we are discovering that our rosy picture of energy as the Key to Prosperity has omitted a number of serious costs, from geopolitical instability and oil price volatility to, now, rising global temperatures due to centuries of carbon dioxide emissions."[2]

Nevertheless, those costs are real. During the 1990s, Jane Ogden at the University of California–Davis calculated that a car with the most efficient internal combustion engine still generated $846 in costs resulting from global warming. Currently, neither the manufacturer of the car nor the person who buys it has to pay those costs. It is for that reason that the drafters of the Kyoto Protocol created a cap-and-trade system. Such an approach would control carbon emissions and pollution by providing economic incentives for achieving reductions in emissions. In Europe, where there is a market for emissions allowances, the right to emit 1 ton (0.9 metric tons) of carbon was trading in the $16 to $24 range in early 2008.

There are other reasons why the government should intervene. One is "regulatory certainty." Business executives believe that the government will someday limit emissions. But until they know how much those limits will cost them, they will postpone decisions about investing in pollution-emitting equipment.

Executives also need to know when emissions limits will take effect. In private conversations, several oil company executives told author Ross Gelbspan that it was possible to "de-carbonize" their energy supplies in an orderly fashion, but they needed the world's governments to regulate the process so that all companies could make the transition at the same time without losing business to competitors. Government can also encourage businesses to develop technology whose financial rewards are too uncertain or too remote for businesses to pursue on their own. Finally, the government can prod individuals into changing their behavior. Mayer Hillman, Tina Fawcett, and Sudhir Chella Rajan observe: "Given the fact that the public is addicted to energy-intensive lifestyles and given the evidence that, at present, it is not prepared of its own volition to give these up to the degree that is so obviously essential, only government can intervene effectively."[3]

The longer we wait, the more global warming will cost.

Hurricane Katrina, which caused more than $80 billion in damage, was a striking example of how much extreme weather can cost us. Those costs will grow as extreme weather becomes more common. The Intergovernmental Panel on Climate Change (IPCC) concluded that there is a better than 90 percent chance that heat waves and heavy precipitation will become more frequent, and better than two chances in three that hurricanes and typhoons will become more intense in the years to come. The IPCC also concluded: "Unmitigated climate change would, in the long term, be *likely* to exceed the capacity of natural, managed and human systems to adapt. Reliance on adaptation alone could eventually lead to a magnitude of climate change to which effective adaptation is not possible, or will only be available at very high social, environmental and economic costs."[4]

Recently, the British government asked Sir Nicholas Stern, a former chief economist at the World Bank, to prepare a report on the economics of climate change. Stern concluded that unchecked global warming would cripple the world's economies: "Using the results from formal economic models, the Review estimates that if we don't act, the overall costs and risks of climate change will be equivalent to losing at least 5% of global GDP [gross domestic product, the total value of goods and services a country produces] each year, now and forever. If a wider range of risks and impacts is taken into account, the estimates of damage could rise to 20% of GDP or more."[5]

In addition to the out-of-pocket costs, there are unquantifiable effects of global warming, such as the thousands of people who lost their homes to Hurricane Katrina, the loss of plant and animal species, and the increased risk of political instability.

On the other hand, Stern found that reducing emissions to avoid the worst impacts of global warming would cost only one percent of global GDP each year. One percent of this country's gross domestic product is about $138 billion—about what we spend each year on the Iraq war—or $460 for every American. However, those costs will rise with every year that we put off acting. The consulting firm McKinsey and Company explained: "Many of the most economically attractive abatement options we analyzed are 'time perishable': every year we delay producing energy-efficient commercial buildings, houses, motor vehicles, and so forth, the more negative-cost options [those that generate more benefits than costs] we lose. The cost of building energy efficiency into an asset when it is created is typically a fraction of the cost of retrofitting it later, or retiring an asset before its useful life is over."[6] Eventually it will be too late to act, either because we cannot afford to pay the cost of reducing emissions or because the process of warming has become unstoppable.

Reducing greenhouse gas emissions is likely to have benefits that will offset at least some of their costs. That is because the same measures that reduce greenhouse gas emissions could also reduce our dependence on overseas oil and cut down on non-greenhouse pollutants that cost our health-care system billions of dollars. Author Robert Hunter argues that reducing our use of carbon can lead to prosperity, not unemployment and poverty:

> We *could* be logically, intelligently, rationally, wisely going about the business of converting to sustainable energy sources.

Using Cap-and-Trade to Fight Acid Rain

Supporters of a cap-and-trade system for reducing greenhouse gas emissions point to the success of a similar program aimed at reducing emissions of sulfur dioxide, a compound that interacts with moisture in the atmosphere to create acid rain, precipitation that is more acidic than what naturally occurs. Acid rain is deadly to trees, insects, and creatures that live in lakes and rivers.

The term *acid rain* was coined in 1872 by Robert Angus Smith, a British government official who argued that there was a link between industrial pollution and acidic precipitation. However, it was not until the 1960s that scientists figured out how industrial emissions caused damage hundreds of miles away and thousands of feet above sea level.

During the 1980s, coal-fired utilities in the Ohio River valley caused acid rain to fall on the Northeast and Canada. A number of eastern states filed suit against the utilities and passed laws aimed at acid rain. Sulfur dioxide, the main active ingredient, had already been identified by Congress in the Clean Air Act of 1970 as harmful to human health.

The first step toward regulating sulfur emissions was the Convention on Long-Range Trans-Boundary Air Pollution, which went into effect in 1983. This was the first international treaty aimed at limiting air pollution. The countries that signed the treaty, including the United States and Canada, pledged to reduce their emissions by 30 percent.

The next step toward regulating sulfur emissions was the 1990 Clean Air Act Amendments.* Title IV of the act ordered electric utilities, by far the largest emitters of sulfur dioxide, to reduce their emissions by 10 million tons (9 million metric tons) per year by 2010.

Title IV was innovative in two respects. First, it departed from the traditional "command and control" approach in which government regulators told businesses how to reduce pollution and by what amounts, and what technology to use. Instead, it let the market determine how best to reduce sulfur emissions.

The wind turbines could be growing like forests. Solar panels could cover every rooftop. Trains and planes powered by fuel cells could be whizzing along. There would go electric cars instead of gasoline guzzlers. Heat pumps. Geothermal. Tidal power. We could be harnessing it all. We have the gear. We

Utilities were given a number of options, including switching to low-sulfur coal, installing pollution control devices, or shutting down plants.

Second, Title IV established a cap-and-trade system. The Environmental Protection Agency (EPA) gave utility companies an initial supply of "allowances," each of which gave them the right to emit 1 ton (0.9 metric tons) of sulfur. The initial allocation was based on companies' fuel consumption and emissions history. Each year afterward, the EPA auctioned a new supply of allowances. When a utility company emitted a ton of sulfur, one allowance was "retired" and could no longer be used. If a company had leftover allowances, it could either sell them to other companies that were over the limit or put them "in the bank" to be used in the future. Trading in sulfur dioxide rights got fully under way in 1995.

According to the EPA, the nation's largest power plants emitted 8.7 million tons (7.9 million metric tons) of sulfur in 1990, when Congress first mandated a cap. By 1995, when trading in credits began, emissions had fallen to 4.5 million tons (4 million metric tons), even though power generation continued to increase. Observers believe that the cap-and-trade system has exceeded expectations. According to Ricardo Bayon of the New America Foundation: "Before Congress mandated the sulfur dioxide cap, the Edison Electric Institute estimated that it would cost $7.4 billion a year for industry to meet its targets; over the ensuing decade, successive studies by a variety of groups have shown that the real figure is likely to be closer to $870 million a year."** Bayon adds: "The sulfur dioxide market provides a business-friendly, market-oriented, cost-effective model for reducing emissions of carbon dioxide, the gas generally considered to be the main culprit behind global warming."

If Congress adopts a cap-and-trade system for carbon emissions, some anticipate that a huge market for them would develop. Bayon quoted trader Carlton Bartels, who predicted that the carbon dioxide market could be worth tens of billions of dollars, perhaps becoming the world's largest commodities market.

* Public Law 101–549.
**Ricardo Bayon, "Trading Futures in Dirty Air: Here's a Market-based Way to Fight Global Warming," *Washington Post*, August 4, 2001.

could be halfway there by now if the technology had been deployed when it could have been.[7]

For that reason, a growing number of business executives believe they can profit in a future "green" economy.

America must lead the fight against global warming.

If the world is to avoid disastrous global warming, the United States must lead. First of all, if this country fails to take steps to reduce emissions, other countries—especially China and India—will conclude that it makes no economic sense to reduce theirs, either. Unless those countries act, their emissions will eventually cause worldwide emissions to rise, no matter what steps industrialized countries take. It is also important to act because many other countries currently distrust us. We are widely perceived as bad international citizens because of the Bush administration's rejection of the Kyoto Protocol and its opposition to meaningful limits on emissions.

As the world's foremost democracy, this country also has an obligation to set a good example. In a recent column in the *New York Times*, Al Gore explained:

> Here Americans have a special responsibility. Throughout most of our short history, the United States and the American people have provided moral leadership for the world. Establishing the Bill of Rights, framing democracy in the Constitution, defeating fascism in World War II, toppling Communism and landing on the moon—all were the result of American leadership.
>
> Once again, Americans must come together and direct our government to take on a global challenge. American leadership is a precondition for success.[8]

Our actions would have powerful symbolic value, reminding other countries that we now live in a carbon-constrained world.

Furthermore, global warming requires concerted action by the world community. Kevin Conrad, who represented the Pacific nation of Papua New Guinea, told fellow delegates at the 2007 climate change meeting in Bali: "I think collectively we as humanity have become more mature in this climate battle, and we understand collectively that we've got to turn off all the emissions sources in order to win. . . . The climate doesn't know whether it came from a factory or from Papua New Guinea's deforestation. We've really got to get all hands on deck and tackle all of the issues." [9] The fight against global warming cannot go forward without the participation of the United States, the world's number one emitter. This country accounts for about 30 percent of the world's greenhouse gas emissions, six times as much per capita as the world as a whole. At the 1992 Earth Summit at Rio de Janeiro, the world community—including the United States—agreed that industrialized countries were the biggest contributors to global warming and should take the lead in solving it. We have not done so, and citizens of developing countries believe that our government has reneged on its commitment.

Many consider it unjust that the countries least responsible for global warming are most vulnerable to its effects. For example, Africa accounts for less than 3 percent of the world's greenhouse gas emissions. Nevertheless, the continent's 840 million people are among those who face the highest risk of drought and flooding as the result of emissions from the United States and other Western countries. Likewise, flood-prone countries like Bangladesh and island nations that could disappear beneath rising seas find themselves in danger—even though their contribution to global warming has been minimal.

Mayer Hillman and his coauthors reflected on the moral questions raised by our greenhouse gas emissions:

Climate change raises a profound philosophical question about what kind of moral beings we are. On the one hand,

(continues on page 100)

Refuting the Arguments Against Global Warming

The Web site of the attorney general of California answers 12 arguments frequently raised by opponents of measures aimed at curbing global warming. The answers quote from the report of the Intergovernmental Panel on Climate Change and other scientific literature.

1. *Some places on Earth are getting cooler.* Global warming describes the overall trend that scientists have found in average temperatures worldwide. Those temperatures have risen over the past 100 years, and most of the warming has occurred in recent years.

2. *Global temperatures fell in the mid-twentieth century.* That drop was the result of increased industrialization after World War II, which led to increased amounts of soot and aerosol pollutants that, overall, tend to have a cooling effect.

3. *The ice is becoming thicker in some parts of Antarctica.* Coastal regions of the ice sheets in West Antarctica are thinning and contributing to the rise in sea levels.

4. *There were times in the past when the Earth's climate was as warm as or even warmer than today.* The rate at which humans are changing the concentrations of greenhouse gases is unprecedented and far from natural. Furthermore, the Medieval Warm Period was not a worldwide warming trend like that which we are experiencing today.

5. *The climate we are seeing today is merely the result of natural variability.* Reconstructions of past climate show that the second half of the twentieth century was likely the warmest 50-year period in the Northern Hemisphere in the last 1,300 years. The rapid warming we have seen is consistent with scientists' understanding of how the climate should respond to a rapid increase in greenhouse gases rather than natural external factors such as variability in solar output and volcanic activity.

6. *Global warming may be beneficial for humans.* It is true that some regions of the Earth would benefit in the short term from warmer temperatures, but the models used by the Intergovernmental Panel on Climate Change indicate that the more the Earth warms, the more the adverse effects will exceed the beneficial effects.

7. *Natural emissions of carbon dioxide are much greater than those from human activities.* Natural exchanges of carbon dioxide were in balance for many thousands of years before the Industrial Revolution, and the concentration of carbon

dioxide in the atmosphere held steady at about 280 parts per million. Emissions caused by humans, primarily from the burning of fossil fuels, have "unbalanced the carbon budget," causing carbon dioxide concentrations to rise since about 1850.

8. *Higher temperatures are the result of greater solar output during the industrial era.* Although solar irradiance has contributed to higher global average temperatures, that effect is very small compared to human-caused increases in greenhouse gases.

9. *The models that predict future climate change are unreliable.* Even though models can err in simulating small-scale events like clouds and tropical downpours, they are more reliable in simulating temperatures. When the results of modeling are compared to observed temperatures, there is very close agreement between them.

10. *Weather forecasts are not accurate for more than a few days ahead. Therefore, it is impossible to predict the future climate.* Just as it is easier to predict the distribution of one million throws of the dice than the result of one individual throw, it is easier to predict long-term variations resulting from changes in the atmosphere than to predict weather patterns days or weeks ahead.

11. *Scientists exaggerate the evidence by linking global warming to events like Hurricane Katrina.* Actually, climate scientists have not blamed global warming for Hurricane Katrina or any other specific weather event. There is, however, a complex relationship between changes in climate and local weather events—including extreme weather—and scientists believe that warmer temperatures will lead to more frequent and more severe extreme weather events.

12. *We should not act until there is 100 percent scientific certainty about global warming.* In science, there is no such thing as 100 percent certainty so demanding certainty is demanding the impossible. According to the attorney general's Web site, "As a society, we make decisions to guard against the risk of future harm every day. We regulate air and water pollutants without waiting for dead bodies. We require safety precautions for dams and nuclear power plants to protect us against low probability but potentially catastrophic accidents. We purchase insurance to guard against uncertain risks from floods, hurricanes, and fires. We do so because waiting until every last doubt is resolved may very well be too late."

Source: Office of the Attorney General of California, "Global Warming Contrarians and the Falsehoods They Promote." http://ag.ca.gov/globalwarming/contrarians.php.

(continued from page 97)

we could leave behind for our children and grandchildren a world that is rendered virtually uninhabitable for most and a correspondingly bleak set of social institutions. A small minority of powerful and wealthy individuals will probably try to secure higher ground and resources and build walls

Chlorofluorocarbons and International Action to Control Them

During the 1930s, scientists developed artificial chemicals called chlorofluorocarbons (CFCs) as an alternative to the sometimes toxic and explosive chemicals that were used in refrigeration. What they did not realize was that CFCs, which are also greenhouse gases, released chlorine that broke down the Earth's ozone layer that protects humans from cancer-causing ultraviolet radiation.

During the 1970s, Frank Sherwood Rowland and Mario Molina, two chemists at the University of California–Irvine, discovered that CFC molecules were stable enough to remain in the atmosphere until they got up into the middle of the stratosphere where, decades later, they would be broken down by ultraviolet radiation and release chlorine atoms. The chlorine atoms, in turn, would break down the ozone in the stratosphere. (Rowland and Molina won the 1995 Nobel Prize for Chemistry for their work on this problem.) Nevertheless, CFC manufacturers such as DuPont disputed the link between CFCs and ozone depletion and resisted mandatory limits.

In 1985, three British scientists published the results of a study in the journal *Nature* that showed that an "ozone hole" had developed over the Antarctic faster than anticipated. That frightening discovery spurred the international community to agree to the 1987 Montreal Protocol on Substances That Deplete the Ozone Layer. The agreement obligated countries that signed it—24 at first—to freeze their CFC use at 1986 levels by 1989 and to cut consumption in half by the end of the twentieth century.

Because ozone depletion affects the planet as a whole, the drafters of the Montreal Protocol used a carrot-and-stick approach to get all countries to cut CFCs. It provided for trade sanctions against noncomplying countries, but on around themselves, putting the poor and weak in greater misery than ever before.[10]

In addition, many people consider it unethical, if not immoral, to make future generations suffer for the consequences of an emissions-heavy lifestyle—especially considering that we can

---

the other hand, offered financial incentives for countries that did sign. In the years that followed, all but a handful of countries signed the protocol, which has been amended a number of times to tighten the restrictions on CFCs. Since the Montreal Protocol came into effect, the atmospheric concentrations of the most important CFCs have either leveled off or fallen.

Climate activists argue that if the world could agree to limit CFCs, it can do the same with greenhouse gases. Matthew Follett, the cofounder of the Green House Network, remarked: "We enacted the Montreal Protocol to reduce the release of chlorofluorocarbons into the atmosphere with far less consensus than we've got on this issue. A third less science than this, and much less consensus."* On the other hand, Ben Lieberman of the Competitive Enterprise Institute disputes the treaty's benefits:

- the threat posed by ozone depletion was far less serious and imminent than originally stated, thus the benefits of the Montreal Protocol are considerably lower;

- the costs of implementing the Protocol's provisions have been, and continue to be, substantial;

- global compliance has been inconsistent."**

Lieberman also warned that the costs of complying with Kyoto would be even higher than those of complying with the Montreal Protocol.

* Katharine Mieszkowski, "The Triumph of Fringe Science," Salon.com, August 7, 2003. http://dir.salon.com/story/tech/feature/2003/08/07/global_warming/index.html
** Ben Lieberman, "Doomsday Déjà Vu: Ozone Depletion's Lessons for Global Warming, 1998. http://cei.org/gencon/025,01184.cfm.

change our behavior at a relatively small cost and without significant disruption to our daily lives.

The world has met other environmental challenges.

Supporters of Kyoto cite two precedents for effective global action on environmental problems: the 1983 Convention on Long-Range Trans-boundary Air Pollution and the 1987 Montreal Protocol on Substances That Deplete the Ozone Layer.

Sulfur was one substance covered by trans-boundary air pollution treaty. The countries that signed the treaty, including the United States and Canada, agreed to cut their emissions by 30 percent. At the time, coal-fired utilities in the Ohio River valley were emitting sulfur that caused acid rain that killed plant and animal life in the Northeast and Canada. In 1990, Congress amended the Clean Air Act. One part of the legislation set national targets for sulfur emissions and also created an innovative way for emitters to reduce them. Lawmakers instructed the Environmental Protection Agency to allocate rights to emit sulfur among utility companies and to establish a mechanism by which companies could buy and sell those rights. This cap-and-trade system proved to be a bigger-than-expected success. When the legislation first passed, an electric utility industry association estimated that it would cost $7.4 billion a year for companies to comply. However, studies by a variety of groups found that the cost was only about $870 million a year.

The Montreal Protocol resulted from the discovery that chlorofluorocarbons (CFCs), which are used in refrigeration, were destroying the ozone layer that keeps ultraviolet radiation from reaching the Earth's surface. Exposure to ultraviolet radiation causes cancer in humans. After a team of scientists discovered a huge hole in the ozone over the Antarctic, the international community moved quickly: Delegates from 24 countries signed the Montreal Protocol, under which they agreed to phase out the production of CFCs. In the years that followed, all but a handful of countries have signed. Kofi Annan, the former secretary general of the United Nations, called the Montreal Protocol perhaps the single most successful international agreement to date. Vijay Vaitheeswaran explains why this treaty is relevant to the fight against global warming:

> Then, as now, some early but inconclusive signs emerged that human actions . . . had unwittingly been contributing to an environmental problem. Then, as now, there was the threat of a disastrous outcome if the problem was ignored. Then, as now, the first impulse of powerful industry interests was to resist forceful action. Then, as now, the chief problem was that only a concerted global response would do: action by the rich world alone could eventually have been undermined by emissions from China and India.[11]

Summary

Global warming is so complex and urgent a problem that we cannot afford to wait for market forces to solve it. The first step government must take is to put a "price tag" on greenhouse gases to force emitters to account for them. Because global warming is a worldwide threat, nothing less than concerted international action can solve it. If the world acts now, it can avoid disastrous consequences at relatively low cost. Global warming raises issues of global justice because the poorest countries are least at fault but stand to suffer its worst effects. The United States, as the world's only superpower and the biggest emitter, has a moral obligation to take the lead in reducing emissions. The international community has acted before, and has done so successfully, to avert threats to the environment.

Kyoto-type Regulation Will Do More Harm than Good

The European Union, a 27-member political and economic alliance of European states, agreed to join the Kyoto Protocol and established a cap-and-trade system aimed at cutting greenhouse gas emissions. Some observers believe that it has been a failure. Kyle Wingfield, an editorial page writer for the *Wall Street Journal Europe*, wrote: "Since 2000, emissions of CO_2 have been growing more rapidly in Europe, with all its capping and yapping, than in the U.S., where there has been minimal government intervention so far. As of 2005, we're talking about a 3.8% rise in the EU-15 versus a 2.5 percent increase in the U.S., according to statistics from the United Nations."[1] The Competitive Enterprise Institute's Christopher Horner adds: "The result [of cap-and-trade] is massive energy cost increases, and industry (jobs) fleeing, with even the alarmists seeking to find a way to stop the capital flight."[2] Given Europe's experience, many believe that Kyoto-type emissions limits would be a drag on America's economy.

The Kyoto Protocol is unfair to the United States.

Many Americans believe that President Bush acted wisely in keeping this country out of Kyoto. To begin with, the treaty does nothing to regulate emissions from developing countries. China is of particular concern because its government has adopted a "growth at any cost" policy that has serious environmental consequences. Mark Lynas explains:

> A fifth of the country's native biodiversity is now endangered. Three-quarters of its lakes are polluted by agricultural or industrial run-off, whilst the Yellow River is depleted and virtually toxic along much of its lower reaches. Almost all China's coastal waters are polluted by sewage, farm pesticides and oil spills, causing on average 90 poisonous red tides per year. Approximately 15,000 square kilometres of grasslands are annually degraded by overgrazing and drought. Acid rain falls on a quarter of its cities. Three out of four urban residents breathe air which falls below minimum health standards.[3]

Perhaps worst of all, China burns huge amounts of coal and uses cheap, high-polluting technology to burn it. Reliance on coal is a major reason why China is already the world's number two greenhouse gas emitter and could overtake the United States in the near future. Additionally, requiring U.S. manufacturers to use clean-fuel technology makes it all the more difficult to compete with cheap imported goods from China.

In addition, Kyoto's emissions targets unfairly favor Europe. Christopher Horner observes that the treaty allowed Europe to create a collective "bubble" under which most countries could take advantage of previous reductions made by Britain and Germany—which happened before Kyoto and were completely unrelated to the treaty. During the 1980s, British prime minister

Why President Bush Rejected the Kyoto Protocol

On March 13, 2001, President George W. Bush wrote a letter to four Republican members of the U.S. Senate on the subject of global warming in general and the Kyoto Protocol in particular. The following are excerpts from his letter:

> As you know, I oppose the Kyoto Protocol because it exempts 80 percent of the world, including major population centers such as China and India, from compliance, and would cause serious harm to the U.S. economy. The Senate's vote, 95–0 [in favor of the Byrd-Hagel Resolution, passed in 1997], shows that there is a clear consensus that the Kyoto Protocol is an unfair and ineffective means of addressing global climate change concerns.
>
> As you also know, I support a comprehensive and balanced national energy policy that takes into account the importance of improving air quality. Consistent with this balanced approach, I intend to work with the Congress on a multipollutant strategy to require power plants to reduce emissions of sulfur dioxide, nitrogen oxides, and mercury. Any such strategy would include phasing in reductions over a reasonable period of time, providing regulatory certainty, and offering market-based incentives to help industry meet the targets. I do not believe, however, that the government should impose on power plants mandatory emissions reductions for carbon dioxide, which is not a "pollutant" under the Clean Air Act.
>
> A recently released Department of Energy Report, "Analysis of Strategies for Reducing Multiple Emissions from Power Plants," concluded that including caps on carbon dioxide emissions as part of a multiple emissions strategy would lead to an even more dramatic shift from coal to natural gas for electric power generation and significantly higher electricity prices compared to scenarios in which only sulfur dioxide and nitrogen oxides were reduced....
>
> [W]e will continue to fully examine global climate change issues— including the science, technologies, market-based systems, and innovative options for addressing concentrations of greenhouse gases in the atmosphere. I am very optimistic that, with the proper focus and working with our friends and allies, we will be able to develop technologies, market incentives, and other creative ways to address global climate change.

Source: White House, "Text of a Letter from the President to Senators Hagel, Helms, Craig, and Roberts," March 13, 2001. http://www.whitehouse.gov/news/releases/2001/03/20010314. html.

Margaret Thatcher pushed her country to switch from coal to natural gas as the result of coal miners' strikes, and the German government shut down obsolete, heavy-polluting factories in the former East Germany after the country's reunification in 1990. S. Fred Singer and Dennis Avery add that European governments, which have imposed high taxes on energy for decades, would like to impose a similar burden on the American economy: "For competitive reasons, Europe wanted very much to see the United States and its famous job-creating economy saddled with the same high energy costs that European employers and drivers already paid. (A barrel of oil that has netted the Saudi oil industry $35 has often yielded the British government $150 in taxes—with the taxes sanctified to 'save the planet.')"[4]

Kyoto would be a significant economic drag on this country. According to economists at Wharton Econometric Forecasting Associates, it would eliminate 2.4 million jobs and reduce our gross domestic product by 3.2 percent, or about $300 billion a year—more than we spend on primary and secondary education combined. Kyoto would do additional harm to this country by taking power away from our elected officials and putting it in the hands of regulators who are more accountable to environmental activists than American voters. John Christy said: "Add to the problems of Kyoto the thorny notions of sovereignty and self-determination. Will the United States surrender any of its sovereignty to an international treaty developed largely by unelected bureaucrats for at best a minuscule result based on uncertain theories?"[5]

Kyoto is government-imposed rationing.

The world needs better technology to reduce greenhouse gas emissions, and the best way to develop that technology is to give business owners an incentive to do so. John Christy observes: "Clever people will develop cheaper ways to create energy with less carbon. Wealthy countries can afford to search for these new sources of energy. The next innovation will come from inventors who want to be rich or famous or accomplished, not by decrees from legislative bodies."[6] Government officials have no incentive—and in any event, lack the skills—to develop new technology.

Kyoto focuses on reducing consumption, not developing new technology, and relies on mandatory limits rather than incentives. Christopher Horner calls Kyoto a form of rationing, plain and simple: "Given foreseeable technologies cutting emissions means rationing energy use, which the greens have long seen as the enemy. . . . Indeed, it is the greens who persistently doubt Man's innovativeness, arguing since the early twentieth century through today's climate models that Man will continue to use today's technology far into the future."[7]

THE LETTER OF THE LAW

The Byrd-Hagel Resolution

Public Law 105–54

As members of Congress learned more about Kyoto Treaty, they became increasingly concerned over its effect on our economy. In July 1997, five months before Kyoto was ratified, Senators Robert Byrd, a Democrat from West Virginia, and Chuck Hagel, a Republican from Nebraska, introduced a "sense of the Senate" resolution that expressed opposition to the proposed treaty. The so-called Byrd-Hagel Resolution (Public Law 105–54) passed by a vote of 95 to 0.

The resolution called the exemption of developing countries "inconsistent with the need for global action on climate change" and "environmentally flawed." It also stated that exempting those countries "could result in serious harm to the United States economy, including significant job loss, trade disadvantages, [and] increased energy and consumer costs." It went on to state that:

(1) the United States should not be a signatory to any protocol to, or other agreement regarding, the United Nations Framework Convention on Climate Change of 1992, at negotiations in Kyoto in December 1997, or thereafter, which would—

(A) mandate new commitments to limit or reduce greenhouse gas emissions for the Annex I Parties, unless the protocol or other agreement also mandates new

Critics add that Kyoto would reverse a decades-long trend toward lifting regulations on business and put government planners back in control of economy. In the past, "top-down" planning has often led to regulations that discouraged innovation and programs that funneled money to projects that made no economic sense. Kyoto could impose top-down planning on a worldwide scale. Furthermore, emissions-reduction measures could seriously diminish the quality of Americans' lives. S. Fred Singer and Dennis Avery explain:

> Kyoto members would have to politically ration the lighting, heating, and refrigeration for their homes, schools, hospitals, factories, and businesses. Transportation for manufactured

---

specific scheduled commitments to limit or reduce greenhouse gas emissions for Developing Country Parties within the same compliance period, or

(B) would result in serious harm to the economy of the United States; and

(2) any such protocol or other agreement which would require the advice and consent of the Senate to ratification should be accompanied by a detailed explanation of any legislation or regulatory actions that may be required to implement the protocol or other agreement and should also be accompanied by an analysis of the detailed financial costs and other impacts on the economy of the United States which would be incurred by the implementation of the protocol or other agreement.*

In spite of the Senate's action, President Clinton sent Vice President Al Gore to the negotiations in Kyoto and later signed the protocol itself. However, his signature had no legal effect because Article II, Section 2 of the U.S. Constitution provides that the ratification of a treaty requires a two-thirds vote of the Senate. Facing strong opposition to Kyoto in the Senate, Clinton never submitted it for ratification. President George W. Bush, Clinton's successor, cited the Byrd-Hagel Resolution as one of the reasons for not ratifying the treaty.

* The Byrd-Hagel Resolution, Public Law 105–54, Available online at http://thomas.loc.gov/ cgi-bin/query/D?c105:1:./temp/~c105P0dAbr::

goods and off-season fresh fruits and vegetables would be sharply curtailed. Tourism might be possible only for the winners of a "travel lottery." Standards of living would plummet, with far fewer good jobs, fewer attractive lifestyle choices, and fewer ways to improve human health.[8]

Some advocates of free markets see government regulators as an even bigger threat than global warming itself.

Finally, Kyoto's drafters were too ambitious. They set out to change the industrialized world's energy-use patterns in 15 years, about as long as it takes a city to prepare for the Olympic Games. That is far from enough time to redesign an energy infrastructure that is currently designed around fossil fuels. Thus there is the danger that government officials will act hastily and commit their countries' economies to costly and inefficient technology. Patrick Michaels and his coauthors observe: "Beyond 50 years, we have little, if any, idea what the energy infrastructure of our society will be. To highlight the folly of any such projection, compare the energy-related concerns of 1900, when pundits cautioned that major U.S. cities would be knee-deep in horse 'emissions' by 1930 unless we saw fit to 'act now,' with those of 2000. We simply cannot predict our future."[9]

Kyoto is unworkable.

A key provision of the Kyoto Protocol is a cap-and-trade system. Some, however, doubt whether such a system could be implemented on a worldwide basis. David Victor, a professor at Stanford University, argues: "Trading of carbon permits across borders rests on international law, which is a weak force. Nations can withdraw if their allocation proves inconvenient, and there are few strong penalties available under international law that can keep them from defecting. Yet the integrity of an emission trading system requires the impossible: that major players not withdraw."[10] Regulating emissions on a global scale also would require developing countries to create political institutions that currently do not exist.

Furthermore, it is too easy for dishonest emitters to cheat under a cap-and-trade system. Ross Gelbspan argues: "[I]nternational carbon trading turned out to be a shell game. Carbon is burned in far too many places—vehicles, factories, homes, fields—to effectively track even if there were an international monitoring system. Trading also became a huge source of contention between industrial and developing countries."[11] Officials at the United Nations recently expressed concern that unscrupulous investors have been receiving Kyoto credits, which they can resell, for their funding of projects that actually do little to reduce emissions. Some Kyoto critics believe that business owners in developing countries have deliberately stepped up their emissions in the hope that investors will pay them to emit less and in the process earn Kyoto credits that can be resold to others. Incidents such as these could undermine confidence in the entire system.

Kyoto, like other regulatory schemes, could be exploited by special interests. Enron Corporation, the notorious energy-trading company that went bankrupt in 2002, was one business that stood to gain from the treaty's adoption. Christopher Horner quoted from a memo written by a lobbyist who called Kyoto "precisely what [Enron was] lobbying for" and predicted that "his treaty will be good for Enron stock!"[12] Some also believe that a cap-and-trade system will reward emitters because the value of the allowances given to them would be larger than the costs of reducing their emissions.

Kyoto will impose large costs and yield few benefits.

Bjorn Lomborg argues that Kyoto makes no economic sense: It would impose $5 trillion in costs worldwide but yield only $2 trillion in benefits. So long as Kyoto's costs exceed its benefits, countries like China and India will have no incentive to participate. Furthermore, critics believe that Kyoto will do little to reduce global temperatures. Senator James Inhofe, a critic of the treaty, explains:

> Dr. Tom Wigley, a senior scientist at the National Center for Atmospheric Research, found that if the Kyoto Protocol were fully implemented by all signatories—now I will note here that this next point assumes that the alarmists' science is correct, which of course it is not—if Kyoto were fully implemented it would reduce temperatures by a mere 0.07 degrees Celsius by 2050, and 0.13 degrees Celsius by 2100. What does this mean? Such an amount is so small that ground-based thermometers cannot reliably measure it.[13]

Worse still, Kyoto will do little to reduce the emissions that have been blamed for global warming. At best, the treaty would merely slow the rate at which emissions are increasing because cuts by industrialized countries, which are subject to emissions limits, will be offset by emissions from countries that are exempt.

In any event, there are better investments than a crash program to get emissions down to the Kyoto targets. Lomborg considers it both more effective and more humane to help the developing world adapt to global warming. For example, assuming that global warming will melt the world's glaciers, it is not expected to happen for at least 50 years. Thus it makes more sense to invest in better water-storage capability for the long term than to meet short-term emissions reduction targets that will not stop the glaciers from melting. Lomborg adds that there are a host of investments that offer a better return than reducing emissions now. The economists who took part in his Copenhagen Consensus Center concluded that stopping the spread of diseases, providing the poor with better food and water, and eliminating trade barriers that drive up the price of necessities, were all "very good" opportunities—investments whose benefits exceeded their costs. By contrast, meeting the Kyoto targets was judged a "bad" opportunity.

Kyoto will hurt the poor.

Billions of people living in developing countries rely on wood, straw, and animal dung to cook food and heat their homes. Using these primitive fuels is not only unhealthy but results in environmental damage, including the loss of forests. Kyoto does nothing to relieve poverty, which John Christy calls "the worst polluter." Kyoto's cap-and-trade system is also unfair to poor countries because it allows rich industrialized countries to buy an unlimited number of credits and "put them in the bank" to be used in the future. Ross Gelbspan explains: "This means that when developing countries eventually become obligated to cut their own emissions, they will be left with only the most expensive options since the cheaper offsets will have already been bought up by industrial countries. This clearly constitutes a form of environmental colonialism."[14]

In this country, Kyoto-type measures will have their greatest effect on less well-off Americans. According to economists at Wharton Economic Forecasting Associates (WEFA): "Because of Kyoto, American consumers would face higher food, medical, and housing costs—for food, an increase of 11%, medicine, an increase of 14%, and housing, an increase of 7%. At the same time an average household of four would see its real income drop by $2,700 in 2010, and each year thereafter."[15]

Critics call Kyoto a tax, and one with greater impact on the poor than on the wealthy. The Congressional Budget Office found: "Regardless of how the allowances were distributed, most of the cost of meeting a cap on CO_2 emissions would be borne by consumers, who would face persistently higher prices for products such as electricity and gasoline. Those price increases would be regressive in that poorer households would bear a larger burden relative to their income than wealthier households would."[16]

The Center for Budget and Policy Priorities adds that energy-related costs would increase as emissions limits grew more stringent. As a result, millions of Americans would fall into poverty, and those who are already poor would stand even less of a chance of escaping poverty. Furthermore, the Congressional Budget Office found that Kyoto would have a negative effect on working families, with those who work in energy-intensive industries like coal mining being most vulnerable to job losses. In the end, a small number of households would bear a large burden.

Summary

Throughout history, government planners have tried, and usually failed, to solve economic and technological problems. Kyoto-type measures that order countries to reduce emissions are likely to fail as well. The structure of the Kyoto Protocol is also flawed: It discriminates against the United States, it is hard to enforce, and it will not stop countries like China from increasing their emissions. Kyoto would impose heavy costs on industrialized countries, especially this one, but at the same time, it would have little impact on global temperatures. The costs of Kyoto would fall most heavily on the poor, both in this country and abroad. Money spent on short-term emissions cuts would be better invested in solutions to problems such as AIDS and other diseases and in improving living standards in developing countries.

Dealing with Global Warming

Mark Hertsgaard, a reporter at *Time* magazine, summed up the problem of global warming: "The latest science makes it clear that we will be living with global warming for the rest of our lives. That's not a happy thought, but it's not necessarily dire either. The key is to follow the new rules of life under global warming. Think ahead, adapt as necessary and make sure to cut greenhouse emissions in time. Adaptation won't be cheap. It won't be optional either."[1] Nevertheless, Americans remain divided over what ought to be done about global warming. Those divisions are likely to persist for years to come.

America's Policy Toward Global Warming

Shortly after taking office, President Bush made it clear that he would keep the United States out of the Kyoto Protocol. His stance offended much of the international community and many Americans as well. However, the president defended his administration's record on climate:

> We believe we need to protect our environment. We believe we need to strengthen our energy security. We believe we need to grow our economy. And we believe the only way to achieve these goals is through continued advances in technology. So we've pursued a series of policies aimed at encouraging the rise of innovative as well as more cost-effective clean energy technologies that can help America and developing nations reduce greenhouse gases, reduce our dependence on oil, and keep our economies vibrant and strong for decades to come.[2]

Before leaving office in January 2009, President Bush announced a new national goal of stopping the growth of greenhouse gas emissions by 2025. Supporters of his approach argued that it is in fact possible to reduce emissions without resorting to Kyoto's inflexible approach. Critics, however, questioned why this country should wait until 2025 to reduce its emissions when other countries are already starting to reduce theirs.

So far, Congress has not passed significant climate legislation. In 2003, the Senate considered, but rejected, a bill[3] that would have reduced emissions to 2000 levels by the year 2010 and imposed a cap-and-trade system to bring that about. In the years that followed, senators voted down several similar bills. The most recent version[4] would have reduced emissions 15 percent by 2020 and 70 percent by 2050. However, the bill was pulled from the Senate floor in June 2008 when it became clear that it would not pass. Opponents argued that cap-and-trade would drive up the price of most goods and services, raise trillions of dollars in tax revenue that government officials might waste on ill-advised projects, and yet have no significant effect on emissions. Nevertheless, many observers believe that comprehensive climate legislation will soon pass. During the 2008 presidential election, both major-party nominees, John McCain and Barack

What Is Contraction and Convergence?

In 1990, a group of activists led by Aubrey Meyer founded the Global Commons Institute (GCI). Its objective is to find a solution to global warming that is fair to all inhabitants of the Earth. A GCI publication, *Contraction and Convergence: A Global Solution to a Global Problem*, states: "Because everyone—regardless of status—is now increasingly vulnerable to the impacts of climate change, the rich have little choice but to share the burden of contraction fairly."

The GCI presented its original agenda to the Second World Climate Conference in 1990. Later, at the urging of the Intergovernmental Panel on Climate Change, it developed a plan that is now known as "Contraction & Convergence" (C&C). The goal of C&C is to reverse the current state of affairs in which industrialized countries account for a growing share of emissions. Developing countries suffer most of the effects of global warming, and the two sides cannot agree on how to solve the problem. The institute observed: "We consider that a failure to face and secure a global commitment of this kind will result in a perpetual stalemate in the international political process to the extent that the agreement and delivery of global abatement targets will become less and less possible."

The "contraction" portion of C&C refers to setting an emissions "budget" that would stabilize the concentration of carbon dioxide in the atmosphere at a safe level by 2100. The institute's original target was 450 parts per million (ppm). However, in light of recent scientific research, and the fact that the world is already feeling the effects of global warming at current concentrations, the institute suggests that the target might have to be lowered to 350 ppm—or even 280 ppm, where it was at the beginning of the Industrial Revolution. To get the carbon dioxide concentration to a safe level and keep it there, it will be necessary to reduce emissions substantially below current levels.

The "convergence" portion of C&C deals with how the right to emit carbon is allocated worldwide. At first, the distribution of these rights would be based on how much each country currently emits. Over time, however, the right to emit would converge toward equal amounts per person worldwide. The year when convergence occurs would be negotiated by the world community. The GCI originally suggested 2045, the centennial of the founding of the United Nations, but it concedes that convergence might not occur until 2100. Even after convergence occurs, the amount of allowable emissions would continue to decline.

Source: Global Commons Institute, *Contraction and Convergence: A Global Solution to a Global Problem*. http://www.gci.org.uk.

Obama, supported some form of cap-and-trade legislation as well as substantial emissions reductions by the middle of this century.

In the meantime, states and cities are taking action against global warming. The most ambitious legislation so far is the California Global Warming Solutions Act of 2006.[5] The act orders a 10 percent reduction in greenhouse gas emissions by 2020 and authorizes cap-and-trade as one way to achieve it. Lawmakers consider it a first step toward meeting the state's commitment to an 80 percent reduction of emissions from 1990 levels by the year 2050. California, which has long been a leader in air-quality legislation, has also moved to limit greenhouse gas emissions from cars and trucks. However, the proposed limits were blocked by the Bush administration. If the next administration allows California to go ahead with those limits, the auto industry will likely challenge them in court. Meanwhile, in the Northeast and the West, some states have created voluntary cap-and-trade programs and have set emissions-reduction goals. In addition, a growing number of states have adopted Renewable Portfolio Standards (RPS) programs, which require utilities to generate part of their electricity from renewable sources such as wind power and solar energy. According to the Renewable Energy Policy Product, 16 states now have RPS in place. However, some believe that RPS requirements allow politicians to make business decisions best left to utility company executives.

At the local level, hundreds of cities have taken steps to reduce their emissions. Seattle has been in the forefront of local efforts. *Time*'s Jeffrey Kluger explains:

> Mayor Greg Nickels . . . who was incensed after the Senate walked away from the international Kyoto global-warming accords, began what has become a nationwide movement to bring U.S. cities into compliance. As of [March 2007], 431 mayors representing more than 61 million Americans had signed on, imposing higher parking taxes, buying hybrid

vehicles for the municipal fleet, helping local businesses audit their energy use and even converting traffic lights from incandescents to LEDs, which are 90% more efficient.[6]

Businesses, too, have started to address the problem. At the 2000 World Economic Forum in Davos, Switzerland, business leaders called climate change the greatest threat facing the world. Since then, a number of corporations have joined forces with environmental groups to find ways to reduce emissions. One such alliance is the U.S. Climate Action Program (USCAP), which favors a regulated economy-wide, market-driven approach to protecting the climate. Many believe that market forces will lead to a solution to global warming, just as they led to oil replacing coal as our principal source of energy. Fred Krupp, the president of the Environmental Defense Fund, recently said: "Global warming skeptics notwithstanding, fixing global warming won't be a drain on the economy. On the contrary, it will unleash one of the greatest floods of new wealth in history. When Congress finally acts, America's entrepreneurs and inventors will find the capital they need to solve global warming—and a lot of people will make a killing."[7] Despite Krupp's optimism, some climate activists fear that alliances like USCAP will put corporate profits ahead of saving the planet.

Strategies for Reducing Emissions

While discussing global warming, President Bush said: "There are only two ways to stabilize concentration of greenhouse gases. One is to avoid emitting them in the first place; the other is to try to capture them after they're created. And there are problems with both approaches."[8] With respect to reducing emissions, the consulting firm McKinsey and Company has identified five "clusters" of initiatives which, if pursued together, could reduce the nation's carbon emissions, which currently total about 7.2 billion tons (6.5 billion metric tons) a year, by between 3 billion and 4.5 billion tons (2.7 billion and 4 billion metric tons) per year. A significant part of those reductions, more than 700 million tons (635 million metric tons), could be brought about by installing more efficient heating and air conditioning in buildings and setting higher performance standards for appliances and electronic devices. These steps are attractive because they are "negative cost" options, meaning that their benefits are greater than their costs. Reductions beyond that, however, would impose costs. For example, switching to more fuel-efficient vehicles and less carbon-intensive fuels would save millions of tons of emissions, but would require automakers to make up-front investments that would be passed along to car buyers in the form of higher prices. The largest reductions, 800 million to more than 1.5 billion tons (726 million to 1.4 billion metric tons), would require the electric power industry to make the transition from fossil fuels to renewable sources. Further reductions could be achieved through "carbon capture and storage": sending carbon emissions to some destinations other than the atmosphere. However, this technology is not yet operational and is likely to be expensive.

Alternatives to the Kyoto Approach

Even though the Kyoto Protocol does not expire until 2012, it is already too late for this country to meet the treaty's emissions target. Even Al Gore recently conceded that it is time to move on from Kyoto and focus on an agreement that will replace it. The climate-change framework that drew up Kyoto remains in existence, setting the stage for a possible follow-up treaty. At the climate change summit held in 2007, delegates discussed, but did not agree to, an emissions-reduction target of 25 to 40 percent. Some observers believe that the next climate treaty will call for reductions in that range, but over a longer period than Kyoto. Critics, however, warn that "Kyoto II" could lead to permanent energy rationing under the control of UN regulators.

The "carbon tax." Critics found a number of faults with Kyoto's cap-and-trade system: It is too complicated, it is difficult to enforce, and it amounts to a hidden tax on consumers. Some believe that a "carbon tax" on emissions would be more straight-forward and easier to administer. It is similar to "sin taxes" on tobacco that, in theory, allow society to recover the costs such as higher medical bills and lost productivity that result from smoking. David Victor has proposed that we start with a relatively modest tax, on the order of $10 a ton of carbon, which translates into about 10 cents extra per gallon of gasoline. Such a tax would put companies on notice that emissions must be accounted for, yet it would be too small to disrupt the economy. Over time, though, the tax would gradually rise, forcing emitters to make difficult decisions. Paul Roberts explains:

> If, for example, it cost over a hundred dollars for every ton of carbon emitted, utilities might find their older coal-fired power plants were no longer such a bargain and that all at once a portfolio of renewables, gas, and . . . carbon capture was looking cost-effective. Consumption patterns would shift dramatically: as the price of gasoline or coal-fired power rose to reflect carbon capture, consumers and businesses would move toward more efficient cars and appliances.[9]

In July 2008, the Canadian province of British Columbia imposed a carbon tax on most fossil fuels. It started at $10 per ton, and will rise to $30 per ton by 2012. Officials made the carbon tax "revenue neutral," meaning that the revenue raised by the tax would be offset by tax cuts elsewhere, including annual rebates to residents of the province. The rebate addresses concerns that carbon taxes fall more heavily on the poor, who spend a higher percentage of their income on energy.

Contraction and convergence. Some climate activists denounce Kyoto's cap-and-trade approach as "carbon colonialism" because it allows wealthy countries to emit much more carbon per capita than developing countries. A British organization called the Global Commons Institute (GCI) calls this disparity

(continues on page 124)

The California Global Warming Solutions Act of 2006

§§38500–38599, California Health & Safety Code

Section 38500 of the California Global Warming Solutions Act of 2006 (Chapter 488, 2006 Statutes of California, codified as §§38500–38599, California Health & Safety Code) sets out the legislature's findings about global warming. Subsection (c) states that California has long been a national and international leader on energy conservation and environmental stewardship efforts and that this legislation would continue that tradition. Section (d) acknowledges that national and international action is necessary to fully address the global warming problem but asserts that action taken by California would have far-reaching effects by encouraging other states, the federal government, and other countries to act.

The key provision of the act, §38550, requires the state to reduce its greenhouse gas emissions to 1990 levels by the year 2020. Section 38505(g) defines "greenhouse gases" to include carbon dioxide, methane, nitrous oxide, hydrofluorocarbons, perfluorocarbons, and sulfur hexafluoride—the same substances that are listed as greenhouse gases in the Kyoto Protocol.

Although the act took effect January 1, 2007, it will not become fully effective until January 1, 2012, at which time mandatory regulations limiting emissions will be in place. It is also expected that the state will operate a cap-and-trade system. The act designates the California Air Resources Board as the lead agency for enforcing its provisions.

In 2007, the board met its first milestones under the act: it developed a list of early actions to begin sharply reducing greenhouse gas emissions, inventoried emissions that have occurred up to now, and established the 2020 emissions limit. That limit is 10 percent below today's level, or about 30 percent below the expected level in 2020 if the state were to follow a "business-as-usual" approach and do nothing.

Another important step toward drawing up regulations was the issuance of a "scoping plan," a discussion document that outlines the steps to be taken to reduce emissions. In June 2008, the board released a draft of the plan. Key elements include the following:

- Expanding and strengthening existing energy efficiency programs and building and appliance standards.

- Expanding the Renewables Portfolio Standard to 33 percent. In other words, utilities will have to produce 33 percent of their power from renewable sources such as wind, solar, biomass, and geothermal energy.

- Developing a cap-and-trade program that will link with other states and Canadian provinces in the Western Climate Initiative to create a regional emissions market.

- Implementing existing state laws, including the state's clean-car and low-carbon fuel standards.

The board anticipates that its regulations will cover about 85 percent of the state's greenhouse gas emissions. It expects to see the first reductions in emissions, beginning as early as 2010, through "new and existing regulations and other measures." By 2012, it expects the cap-and-trade program to start delivering reductions; and by 2020, cap-and-trade will achieve a significant portion of the reductions required by the act.

Beyond 2020, the board anticipates that a combination of regulations, cap-and-trade, and new technology will meet California's long-term greenhouse gas reduction goals. In Executive Order S-3–05, Governor Arnold Schwarzenegger committed the state to cutting greenhouse gas emissions by 80 percent from 1990 levels by the year 2050.

Critics argue that the legislation is a flawed approach because it will encourage businesses to flee to unregulated states, resulting in serious damage to California's economy. Assuming that action is needed, they urge that it be taken at the national level. Supporters of the legislation argue that it will pay off in the long term. They cite a 2006 report by the University of California–Berkeley, which found that investments in "green" technologies would produce jobs at a higher rate than investments in comparable conventional technologies. They argue that the loss of energy-intensive industries like cement making will be more than offset by clean-technology start-ups.

Source: California Air Resources Board, *Climate Change Draft Scoping Plan: A Framework for Change*. Sacramento, 2008. http://www.arb.ca.gov/cc/scopingplan/document/draftscopingplan.pdf.

(continued from page 121)

unjust. It argues that everyone, regardless of status, is now vulnerable to the effects of global warming, and therefore the rich have no choice but to share the burden of emissions reduction fairly. GCI has offered a long-term program called "contraction and convergence," which Ross Gelbspan explains: "Under the plan, the governments of the world would gradually begin to reduce emissions on a basis that is roughly proportional to their population. If C&C were adopted as the tool for managing CO_2 and other greenhouse gases, 'there would be a transition to a point (convergence) where future entitlements to emit will have become proportional to population,' according to [GCI's founder Aubrey] Meyer."[10]

Another proposal under consideration is called SkyTrust. It is modeled after Alaska's Permanent Fund, which distributes the windfall profits from that state's oil reserves on an equal basis to its residents. SkyTrust is a variation of the cap-and-trade system in which the money paid for the right to emit carbon would be divided among Americans, each of whom would be given one "share" of the atmosphere.

A longer-term approach. Some believe that another major flaw with Kyoto was its short time frame. Vijay Vaitheeswaran argues that a program to reduce emissions must start modestly "because the capital stock involved in the global energy system is vast and long-lived, so a breathless dash to scrap fossil-fuel plans in favor of renewable energy would involve enormous cost."[11] Crash measures aimed at reducing emissions will fail in the long run if countries that act too fast end up bankrupting themselves and thus become unable to pay for longer-term solutions. Robert Socolow, an engineering professor at Princeton University, says: "A 50-year perspective may be best: It is long enough to allow changes in infrastructure and consumption patterns but short enough to be heavily influenced by decisions made today."[12] In 2004, Socolow and his colleagues drew up a strategy that would reduce emissions by nearly 200 billion tons (181 billion metric tons) over a 50-year period and thus stabilize emissions at their current levels. They emphasize that no single strategy can bring about the needed reductions: "Until a few years ago, the environmental community was almost exclusively interested in policies that promote renewable energy, conservation, and natural sinks. More recently, it has begun to explore alliances with traditional energy supply industries on the grounds that to establish the pace required to achieve environmental goals, parallel action on many fronts is required."[13]

The End of Fossil Fuels?

Steve Lohr, a reporter for the *New York Times*, remarked: "In the very long term, environmental experts say, the world's economy needs a technological transformation, from deriving 90 percent of its energy from fossil fuels today to being largely free of emissions from fossil fuels by 2100, through cleanup steps or alternative energy sources."[14] Much has been written about alternatives to oil, gas, and coal as energy sources. Even though alternatives are promising, each has significant drawbacks. Nuclear power requires huge capital investments to build plants; nuclear plants are considered dangerous because of the risk of escaping radiation or fear of a terrorist attack; and few Americans want a plant built near their community. Solar and wind power have reliability problems since solar energy is unavailable at night and the wind does not always blow at the right speed to provide power. Hydrogen power is still in the planning stages, and most current technology uses fossil fuels as part of the process of generating power. In fact, some experts believe that the often touted "hydrogen economy" will never become reality. Finally, alternative sources are still more expensive than fossil fuels; therefore, heavy emitters have no incentive to switch to them.

In 2007, the IPCC concluded: "There is *high agreement* and *much evidence* that all stabilisation levels assessed can be achieved by deployment of a portfolio of technologies that are

(*continues on page 128*)

Mitigation Techniques: Cutting Greenhouse Gas Emissions

There are two ways to combat global warming: *mitigation*, which involves reducing the amount of greenhouse gases we emit into the atmosphere; and *adaptation*, which involves defending against the effects of global warming. One working group of the Intergovernmental Panel on Climate Change (IPCC) focused on mitigation strategies, and its findings were part of the IPCC's *Fourth Assessment Report*. The panel concluded that governments had a wide variety of strategies at their disposal to create incentives for mitigation. It also outlined specific strategies, identified those that were likely to be commercialized by 2030, and suggested how they could be implemented.

With respect to energy supply:

- *Key mitigation technologies* include more efficient supply and distribution; switching from coal to gas; making greater use of nuclear power; making greater use of renewable sources such as hydropower, solar, wind, geothermal, and bioenergy; generating both heat and power at the same site; and carbon capture and storage (CCS), a technology that would store carbon dioxide beneath the Earth's surface rather than releasing it into the atmosphere.

- *Those expected to be commercialized by 2030* include CCS for gas-, biomass-, and coal-fired electricity generating facilities; advanced nuclear power; advanced renewable energy, including tidal and wave energy; and some forms of solar power.

- *Means of implementation* include reducing government subsidies for coal, oil, and gas, and subsidizing renewable energy instead; "feed-in tariffs," which require utilities to buy energy from renewable sources at above-market rates; and requirements that utilities generate a minimum percentage of their energy from renewable sources.

With respect to transport:

- *Key mitigation technologies* include more fuel-efficient vehicles; hybrid vehicles, which are powered by both fossil and non-fossil fuels; cleaner diesel vehicles; biofuels, which are derived from plants; and relying less on cars and trucks and more on public transit, bicycles, and walking.

- *Those expected to be commercialized by 2030* include second-generation biofuels; higher efficiency aircraft; and advanced electric and hybrid vehicles with more powerful and reliable batteries.

- *Means of implementation* include mandatory fuel economy standards; carbon dioxide standards for cars and trucks; higher taxes on vehicles and "road pricing" (higher fees for travel during peak periods and in congested areas); land-use regulation that discourages sprawl; and greater investment in alternatives to automobile travel.

With respect to buildings:

- *Key mitigation technologies* include more efficient lighting, electrical appliances, and heating and cooling devices; better insulation; using solar energy for heating and cooling; alternative refrigeration fluids; and recovery and recycling of fluorinated gases that are used in air conditioning and have high global warming potential.

- *Those expected to be commercialized by 2030* include integrated design of commercial buildings; technologies such as intelligent utility meters that enable users to shift energy consumption to off-peak periods; and equipping buildings with photovoltaics, which convert light directly into heat.

- *Means of implementation* include appliance standards and labeling; government regulation, including building codes and certification; programs to encourage energy efficiency and conservation on the part of building owners; and incentives for utility companies.

With respect to industry:

- *Key mitigation technologies* include recovering more heat and power from machinery; recycling; using materials with less environmental impact; and controlling emissions of gases other than carbon dioxide.

(continues)

(continued)

- *Those expected to be commercialized by 2030* include advanced energy efficiency and CCS for cement, ammonia, and iron manufacture.

- *Means of implementation* include providing information to industrial buyers; setting equipment performance standards; and offering subsidies and tax credits for the use of more efficient and less-polluting equipment.

With respect to agriculture:

- *Key mitigation technologies* include better land management to increase the amount of carbon stored in the soil; restoring degraded lands; better rice cultivation techniques and livestock management to reduce methane emissions; improved ways of applying nitrogen fertilizer to reduce nitrous oxide emissions; the growing of "energy crops" to replace fossil fuel consumption; and improved energy efficiency.

- *Those expected to be commercialized by 2030* include improvements in crop yields.

- *Means of implementation* include financial incentives and regulations to promote better land management; maintaining the soil's carbon content; and more efficient use of fertilizers and irrigation.

With respect to forests and forestry:

- *Key mitigation technologies* include restocking depleted forests; cutting down fewer trees to make room for farmland or human habitation;

(continued from page 125)

either currently available or expected to be commercialised in coming decades, assuming appropriate and effective incentives are in place for their development, acquisition, deployment and diffusion and addressing related barriers."[15] Experts believe that the government can play a role by funding research and development of new technology; granting tax breaks and subsidies to alternative energy sources rather than fossil fuels; enacting management of harvested wood products; and using trees to produce bioenergy and thus replace fossil fuels.

- *Those expected to be commercialized by 2030* include planting tree species that will produce more fuel and absorb more carbon; remote sensing technologies that will analyze the ability of forests to absorb carbon; and mapping changes in land use.

- *Means of implementation* include financial incentives to increase forest area, reduce deforestation, and maintain and manage forests; and better land-use regulation and enforcement.

With respect to waste:

- *Key mitigation technologies* include recovering methane at landfills; burning waste and recovering the energy; composting organic waste; better treatment of wastewater; and recycling more and wasting less.

- *Those expected to be commercialized by 2030* include better technology to prevent methane from escaping from landfills and converting methane into carbon dioxide and water.

- *Means of implementation* include financial incentives for improved waste and wastewater management; renewable energy incentives or requirements; and waste management regulations.

Source: United Nations Intergovernmental Panel on Climate Change, *Fourth Assessment Report. Climate Change 2007: Synthesis Report. Summary for Policymakers*. Geneva, Switzerland, 2007.

"technology-forcing" regulations such as Corporate Fuel Average Economy standards, which resulted in more fuel-efficient cars; and taking the lead in cutting emissions, for example, by using renewable fuels in government vehicle fleets and making energy efficiency a priority in government buildings.

Even though there is reason for optimism, climate activists warn that we cannot wait any longer. A group of researchers led by James Hansen recently said, "The stakes, for all life on the planet, surpass those of any previous crisis. The greatest danger is continued ignorance and denial, which could make tragic consequences unavoidable."[16]

Summary

The Bush administration opposed the Kyoto Protocol as well as federal legislation that would limit greenhouse gas emissions. However, President Obama took office in 2009, making it more likely that some kind of climate legislation will eventually pass. In the meantime, many state and city governments are not waiting for federal action and have taken steps to reduce their own emissions. Kyoto will expire in 2012, and attention is turning to future climate strategy. Some have proposed alternatives to Kyoto's cap-and-trade approach, including a carbon tax, contraction-and-convergence, and multifaceted approaches that emphasize better new energy sources and the development of alternative energy sources. Ultimately, humans may have to abandon fossil fuels entirely, but doing so will require technology that has not yet been developed.

Beginning Legal Research

The goals of each book in the POINT/COUNTERPOINT series are not only to give the reader a basic introduction to a controversial issue affecting society, but also to encourage the reader to explore the issue more fully. This Appendix is meant to serve as a guide to the reader in researching the current state of the law as well as exploring some of the public policy arguments as to why existing laws should be changed or new laws are needed.

Although some sources of law can be found primarily in law libraries, legal research has become much faster and more accessible with the advent of the Internet. This Appendix discusses some of the best starting points for free access to laws and court decisions, but surfing the Web will uncover endless additional sources of information. Before you can research the law, however, you must have a basic understanding of the American legal system.

The most important source of law in the United States is the Constitution. Originally enacted in 1787, the Constitution outlines the structure of our federal government, as well as setting limits on the types of laws that the federal government and state governments can enact. Through the centuries, a number of amendments have added to or changed the Constitution, most notably the first 10 amendments, which collectively are known as the "Bill of Rights" and which guarantee important civil liberties.

Reading the plain text of the Constitution provides little information. For example, the Constitution prohibits "unreasonable searches and seizures" by the police. To understand concepts in the Constitution, it is necessary to look to the decisions of the U.S. Supreme Court, which has the ultimate authority in interpreting the meaning of the Constitution. For example, the U.S. Supreme Court's 2001 decision in *Kyllo v. United States* held that scanning the outside of a person's house using a heat sensor to determine whether the person is growing marijuana is an unreasonable search—if it is done without first getting a search warrant from a judge. Each state also has its own constitution and a supreme court that is the ultimate authority on its meaning.

Also important are the written laws, or "statutes," passed by the U.S. Congress and the individual state legislatures. As with constitutional provisions, the U.S. Supreme Court and the state supreme courts are the ultimate authorities in interpreting the meaning of federal and state laws, respectively. However, the U.S. Supreme Court might find that a state law violates the U.S. Constitution, and a state supreme court might find that a state law violates either the state or U.S. Constitution.

Not every controversy reaches either the U.S. Supreme Court or the state supreme courts, however. Therefore, the decisions of other courts are also important. Trial courts hear evidence from both sides and make a decision, while appeals courts review the decisions made by trial courts. Sometimes rulings from appeals courts are appealed further to the U.S. Supreme Court or the state supreme courts.

Lawyers and courts refer to statutes and court decisions through a formal system of citations. Use of these citations reveals which court made the decision or which legislature passed the statute, and allows one to quickly locate the statute or court case online or in a law library. For example, the Supreme Court case *Brown v. Board of Education* has the legal citation 347 U.S. 483 (1954). At a law library, this 1954 decision can be found on page 483 of volume 347 of the U.S. Reports, which are the official collection of the Supreme Court's decisions. On the following page, you will find samples of all the major kinds of legal citation.

Finding sources of legal information on the Internet is relatively simple thanks to "portal" sites such as findlaw.com and lexisone.com, which allow the user to access a variety of constitutions, statutes, court opinions, law review articles, news articles, and other useful sources of information. For example, findlaw.com offers access to all Supreme Court decisions since 1893. Other useful sources of information include gpo.gov, which contains a complete copy of the U.S. Code, and thomas.loc.gov, which offers access to bills pending before Congress, as well as recently passed laws. Of course, the Internet changes every second of every day, so it is best to do some independent searching.

Of course, many people still do their research at law libraries, some of which are open to the public. For example, some state governments and universities offer the public access to their law collections. Law librarians can be of great assistance, as even experienced attorneys need help with legal research from time to time.

Common Citation Forms

Source of Law	Sample Citation	Notes
U.S. Supreme Court	*Employment Division v. Smith*, 485 U.S. 660 (1988)	The U.S. Reports is the official record of Supreme Court decisions. There is also an unofficial Supreme Court ("S. Ct.") reporter.
U.S. Court of Appeals	*United States v. Lambert,* 695 F.2d 536 (11th Cir.1983)	Appellate cases appear in the Federal Reporter, designated by "F." The 11th Circuit has jurisdiction in Alabama, Florida, and Georgia.
U.S. District Court	*Carillon Importers, Ltd. v. Frank Pesce Group, Inc.,* 913 F.Supp. 1559 (S.D.Fla.1996)	Federal trial-level decisions are reported in the Federal Supplement ("F. Supp."). Some states have multiple federal districts; this case originated in the Southern District of Florida.
U.S. Code	Thomas Jefferson Commemoration Commission Act, 36 U.S.C., §149 (2002)	Sometimes the popular names of legislation—names with which the public may be familiar—are included with the U.S. Code citation.
State Supreme Court	*Sterling v. Cupp*, 290 Ore. 611, 614, 625 P.2d 123, 126 (1981)	The Oregon Supreme Court decision is reported in both the state's reporter and the Pacific regional reporter.
State Statute	Pennsylvania Abortion Control Act of 1982, 18 Pa. Cons. Stat. 3203-3220 (1990)	States use many different citation formats for their statutes.

Cases

Massachusetts v. Environmental Protection Agency, 549 U.S. 497 (2007)
After the Environmental Protection Agency (EPA) decided against regulating
greenhouse gases, the commonwealth of Massachusetts and a group of environmental organizations challenged that decision in court. After hearing the case,
the U.S. Supreme Court ordered the EPA to determine whether greenhouse gases
were dangerous and if so, how they should be regulated.

State of Connecticut v. American Electric Power Company,
406 F. Supp. 2d 265 (S.D.N.Y. 2005)

People of the State of California v. General Motors Corporation,
No. C06–057555 MJJ (U.S. Dist. Ct., N.D. Cal., September 17, 2007)
In these two different lawsuits, state governments tried to hold electric utilities
and automakers accountable for their carbon dioxide emissions. Each lawsuit
was dismissed on the grounds that the elected branches of government, not the
courts, should impose greenhouse gas limits.

Statutes

The Clean Air Act, 42 U.S.C. § 7401 and following (1970)
Congress has amended this law a number of times since its enactment in 1970.
A major amendment in 1990 (Public Law 101–549) established a cap-and-trade
system for emissions that cause acid rain.

The Kyoto Protocol (1997)
International regulation of greenhouse gases is based on Article 2 of the *United
Nations Framework Convention on Climate Change* (UNFCCC), to which most
of the international community agreed in 1992. In Article 2 of the convention,
countries pledged to keep greenhouse gas concentrations at a level that would
prevent dangerous human-caused interference with the Earth's climate system.
The Kyoto agreement resulted from the work of the UNFCCC. It requires the
world's industrialized countries to reduce their emissions to 5.2 percent below
1990 levels by the year 2012. The U.S. Senate never ratified the Kyoto Protocol.

Byrd-Hagel Resolution, Public Law 105–54 (1997)
This resolution expressed the U.S. Senate's opposition to Kyoto on two grounds:
It exempted major emitters such as China and India, and its emissions limits
would cause serious damage to the American economy.

The Global Warming Solutions Act of 2006, Chapter 488, California
Statutes of 2006; codified as §§38500–38599, California Health & Safety
Code (2006)
At the state level, this is the most comprehensive climate legislation thus far. It
requires a reduction in emissions to 1990 levels by the year 2020 and authorizes a
cap-and-trade system to achieve the reduction.

Terms and Concepts

abrupt climate change
adaptation
alternative fuels
anthropogenic
Byrd-Hagel resolution
cap-and-trade
carbon dioxide concentration
carbon sequestration
carbon "sink"
carbon tax
climate models
contraction and convergence
El Niño
emissions trading
energy efficiency
feedback mechanism
fossil fuels
greenhouse effect
greenhouse gases
ice age
Intergovernmental Panel on Climate Change (IPCC)
irreversible climate change
Kyoto Protocol
market forces
mitigation
Modern Warming
natural variability
paleoclimate
pollutants
rationing
solar irradiance
tipping point
United Nations Framework Convention on Climate Change (UNFCCC)

NOTES

Introduction: The Problem of Global Warming

1 Norwegian Nobel Committee, Press Release, "The Nobel Prize for 2007." http://nobelprize.org/nobel_prizes/peace/laureates/2007/press.html.
2 Ibid.
3 Robert Hunter, *Thermageddon: Countdown to 2030*. New York: Arcade Publishing, 2003, p. 40.
4 Peter W. Huber and Mark P. Mills, *The Bottomless Well: The Twilight of Fuel, the Virtue of Waste, and Why We Will Never Run Out of Energy*. New York: Basic Books, 2005, p. 158.
5 Hunter, *Thermageddon*, p. 11.
6 Gale E. Christianson, *Greenhouse: The 200-Year Story of Global Warming*. New York: Walker and Company, 1999, p. 114.
7 Bjorn Lomborg, *Cool It: The Skeptical Environmentalist's Guide to Global Warming*. New York: Alfred A. Knopf, 2007, p. 10.
8 Christianson, *Greenhouse*, pp. 155–56.
9 Al Gore, *An Inconvenient Truth: The Planetary Emergency of Global Warming and What We Can Do About It*. Emmaus, PA: Rodale Press, 2006, p. 38.
10 Climate Research Board, *Carbon Dioxide and Climate: A Scientific Assessment*. Washington, D.C.: National Academies Press, 1979, p. viii.
11 Brian Fagan, *The Little Ice Age: How Climate Made History, 1300–1850*. New York: Basic Books, 2000, pp. 208–9.
12 Ross Gelbspan, *Boiling Point: How Politicians, Big Oil and Coal, Journalists, and Activists Are Fueling the Climate Crisis—and What We Can Do to Avert Disaster*. New York: Basic Books, 2004, p. 154.
13 John Carlisle, *Global Warming: Enjoy It While You Can*. Washington, D.C.: National Center for Public Policy, 1998, http://www.nationalcenter.org/NPA194.html.
14 Ibid.

Point: Human Activity Causes Global Warming

1 Ross Gelbspan, *Boiling Point*, p. 2.
2 Ibid., p. 76.

3 Ibid., p. 28.
4 United Nations Intergovernmental Panel on Climate Change, *Fourth Assessment Report. Climate Change 2007: Synthesis Report. Summary for Policymakers*. Geneva, Switzerland, 2007, p. 39.
5 Ibid., p. 37.
6 Jeffrey Kluger, "What Now for Our Feverish Planet?" *Time*, April 9, 2007, http://www.time.com/time/specials/2007/environment/article/0,28804,1602354_1596572_1604908,00.html.
7 United Nations Intergovernmental Panel on Climate Change, *Fourth Assessment Report*, p. 47.
8 Jim Baker, quoted in Gore, *An Inconvenient Truth*, p. 261.
9 Naomi Oreskes, "The Scientific Consensus on Climate Change," *Science*, December 3, 2004, p. 1686.
10 United Nations Intergovernmental Panel on Climate Change, *Fourth Assessment Report*, p. 30.
11 Gelbspan, *Boiling Point*, pp. 39–40.
12 James Inhofe, Senate Floor Statement, "The Science of Climate Change," *Congressional Record*, July 28, 2003, http://inhofe.senate.gov/pressreleases/climate.htm.
13 Gore, *An Inconvenient Truth*, p. 263.

Counterpoint: Humans Are Not to Blame for Global Warming

1 White House, "President Bush Discusses Climate Change." http://www.whitehouse.gov/news/releases/2001/06/20010611-2.html.
2 John Christy, quoted in Elizabeth Royte, "The Gospel According to John," *Discover*, February 1, 2001, http://discovermagazine.com/2001/feb/featgospel.
3 Christianson, *Greenhouse*, p. 161.
4 S. Fred Singer and Dennis T. Avery, *Unstoppable Global Warming: Every 1,500 Years*. Lanham, Md.: Rowman & Littlefield Publishers, 2007, p. 1.
5 Patrick J. Michaels, *Meltdown: The Predictable Distortion of Global Warming by Scientists, Politicians, and the Media*. Washington, D.C.: Cato Institute, 2004, p. 3.

6 Singer and Avery, *Unstoppable Global Warming*, p. 76.
7 Christopher C. Horner, *The Politically Incorrect Guide to Global Warming and Environmentalism*. Washington, D.C.: Regnery Publishing, 2007, p. 72.
8 Ronald Bailey, ed., *Global Warming and Other Eco-myths: How the Environmental Movement Uses False Science to Scare Us to Death*. Roseville, Calif.: Prima Publishing, 2002, pp. 4–5.
9 Jens Bischof, "Ice in the Greenhouse: Earth May Be Cooling, Not Warming," *Quest*, January 2002, http://www.odu.edu/ao/instadv/quest/Greenhouse.html.
10 Terence Corcoran, "Climate Consensus and the End of Science," *National Post* (Canada), June 12, 2006, http://www.nationalpost.com/news/story.html?id=d35ca1eb-50b8-4546-8950-ca9ad18eb252&p=1.
11 Horner, *The Politically Incorrect Guide to Global Warming and Environmentalism*, p. 3.
12 James Lovelock, quoted in John McCain, Statement Introducing S. 1151, the Climate Stewardship and Innovation Act of 2005, *Congressional Record*, May 26, 2005.

April 24, 2007, http://www.nytimes.com/2007/04/24/opinion/24homer-dixon.html
7 Gelbspan, *Boiling Point*, p. 177.
8 Mark Lynas, *Six Degrees: Our Future on a Hotter Planet*. London: Fourth Estate, 2007, p. 127.
9 Paul Eccleston and Charles Clover, "Global Warming 'Is Happening Faster,'" *Telegraph* (U.K.), October 23, 2007, http://www.telegraph.co.uk/earth/main.jhtml?xml=/earth/2007/10/23/eacarb123.xml.
10 United Nations Intergovernmental Panel on Climate Change, *Fourth Assessment Report*, p. 13.
11 Timothy M. Lenton et al., "Tipping Elements in the Earth's Climate System," *Proceedings of the National Academy of Science*, February 12, 2008, p. 1792.
12 James Hansen et al., *Target Atmosphere CO_2: Where Should Humanity Aim?* New York: Columbia University Earth Institute, 2008, p. 12.
13 Al Gore, "Moving Beyond Kyoto," *New York Times*, July 1, 2007, http://www.nytimes.com/2007/07/01/opinion/01gore.html.

Point: Global Warming Is a Serious Threat

1 Mayer Hillman, Tina Fawcett, and Sudhir Chella Rajan, *The Suicidal Planet: How to Prevent Global Climate Catastrophe*. New York: Thomas Dunne Books, 2007, pp. 25–26.
2 Joseph Romm, "Desperate Times, Desperate Scientists," Salon.com, December 12, 2007.
3 Ibid.
4 Jonathan A. Patz, "Global Warming: Health Impacts May Be Abrupt in the Long Term," *British Medical Journal*, May 29, 2004, p. 1269.
5 Julian Borger, "Darfur Conflict Heralds Era of Wars Triggered by Climate Change, UN Report Warns," *Guardian* (U.K.), June 23, 2007, http://www.guardian.co.uk/environment/2007/jun/23/sudan.climatechange.
6 Thomas Homer-Dixon, "Terror in the Weather Forecast," *New York Times*,

Counterpoint: The Dangers of Global Warming Are Exaggerated

1 Horner, *The Politically Incorrect Guide to Global Warming and Environmentalism*, pp. 67–68.
2 American Association of State Climatologists, *Policy Statement on Climate Variability and Change*, 2001. http://www.stateclimate.org/publications/files/aasclimatepolicy.pdf.
3 Freeman Dyson, quoted in Horner, *The Politically Incorrect Guide to Global Warming and Environmentalism*, p. 113.
4 John Christy, "The Global Warming Fiasco," in Bailey, *Global Warming and Other Eco-myths*, p. 24.
5 R.A. Pielke Jr., C. Landsea, M. Mayfield, J. Laver, and R. Pasch, "Global Warming and Hurricanes," *Bulletin of the American Meteorological Society*, November 2005, p. 1575.
6 Editorial, "Not So Hot," *Wall Street Journal*, August 29, 2007.

7 Bailey, *Global Warming and Other Eco-myths*, p. xxiii.
8 Lomborg, *Cool It*, p. 127.
9 Michaels, *Meltdown*, p. 26.
10 Lomborg, *Cool It*, p. 42.
11 Ibid., p. 79.
12 Singer and Avery, *Unstoppable Global Warming*, p. 17.
13 Carlisle, *Global Warming*, 1998, http://www.enterstageright.com/archive/articles/0598globalwarm.htm.
14 Ibid.

Point: Governments, Including Ours, Must Take Action

1 Vijay V. Vaitheeswaran, *Power to the People: How the Coming Energy Revolution Will Transform an Industry, Change Our Lives, and Maybe Even Save the Planet*. New York: Farrar, Strauss and Giroux, 2003, p. 122.
2 Paul Roberts, *The End of Oil: On the Edge of a Perilous New World*. Boston: Houghton Mifflin, 2004, p. 118.
3 Mayer Hillman with Tina Fawcett and Sudhir Chella Rajan, *The Suicidal Planet: How to Prevent Global Climate Catastrophe*. New York: Thomas Dunne Books, 2007, p. 85.
4 United Nations Intergovernmental Panel on Climate Change. *Fourth Assessment Report*, p. 65.
5 Nicholas Stern, *Stern Review: The Economics of Climate Change. Summary of Conclusions*. London, England: Her Majesty's Treasury, 2006, p. vi.
6 McKinsey and Company, *Reducing U.S. Greenhouse Gas Emissions: How Much and at What Cost? Executive Summary*. New York, 2007, p. xvi.
7 Hunter, *Thermageddon*, p. 270.
8 Gore, "Moving Beyond Kyoto," http://www.nytimes.com/2007/07/01/opinion/01gore.html.
9 Andrew C. Revkin, "Issuing a Bold Challenge to the U.S. Over Climate," *New York Times*, January 22, 2008, http://www.nytimes.com/2008/01/22/science/earth/22conv.html.
10 Hillman with Fawcett and Rajan, *The Suicidal Planet*, p. 5.
11 Vaitheeswaran, *Power to the People*, p. 158.

Counterpoint: Kyoto-type Regulation Will Do More Harm than Good

1 Kyle Wingfield, "Europe's Carbon Con Job," *Wall Street Journal*, August 21, 2007, http://online.wsj.com/article/SB118764555108003341.html.
2 Horner, *The Politically Incorrect Guide to Global Warming and Environmentalism*, p. 258.
3 Lynas, *Six Degrees*, p. 184.
4 Singer and Avery, *Unstoppable Global Warming*, p. 59.
5 Bailey, *Global Warming and Other Eco-myths*, p. 25.
6 Ibid., p. 27.
7 Horner, *The Politically Incorrect Guide to Global Warming and Environmentalism*, pp. 78–79.
8 Singer and Avery, *Unstoppable Global Warming*, pp. 72–73.
9 Patrick J. Michaels, Paul C. Knappenberger, and Robert E. Davis, "The Way of Warming," *Regulation*, Fall 2000, p. 14.
10 Vaitheeswaran, *Power to the People*, p. 146.
11 Ross Gelbspan, "A Modest Proposal to Stop Global Warming," *Sierra*, May 2001, p. 62.
12 Horner, *The Politically Incorrect Guide to Global Warming and Environmentalism*, p. 194.
13 "The Science of Climate Change," Senate Floor Statement by U.S. Senator James Inhofe, Chairman, Committee on the Environment and Public Works, July 28, 2003.
14 Gelbspan, *Boiling Point*, p. 157.
15 "The Science of Climate Change," Senate Floor Statement by U.S. Senator James Inhofe.
16 Congressional Budget Office. *Trade-Offs in Allocating Allowances for CO_2 Emissions*. Washington, D.C., 2007, p. 1.

Conclusion: Dealing with Global Warming

1 Mark Hertsgaard, "On the Front Lines of Climate Change," *Time*, April 9, 2007.
2 White House, "President Bush Discusses Climate Change."

3 Lieberman-McCain Climate Stewardship Act, S. 139, 107th Congress.

4 Climate Security Act of 2007, S. 2191, 110th Congress.

5 Chapter 488, California Statutes of 2006; codified as §§38500–38599, California Health & Safety Code.

6 Kluger, "What Now for Our Feverish Planet?" http://www.time.com/time/specials/2007/environment/article/0,28804,1602354_1596572_1604908,00.html.

7 Fred Krupp, "Climate Change Opportunity," *Wall Street Journal*, April 8, 2008, http://s.wsj.net/public/article_print/SB120761565455196769.html.

8 White House, "President Bush Discusses Global Climate Change."

9 Roberts, *The End of Oil*, p. 276.

10 Gelbspan, *Boiling Point*, p. 159.

11 Vaitheeswaran, *Power to the People*, p. 156.

12 Robert Socolow, Roberta Hotinski, Jeffrey B. Greenblatt, and Stephen Pacala, "Solving the Climate Problem: Technologies Available to Curb CO_2 Emissions," *Environment*, December 2004, p. 8.

13 Ibid.

14 Steve Lohr, "The Cost of an Overheated Planet," *New York Times*, December 12, 2006, http://www.nytimes.com/2006/12/12/business/worldbusiness/12warm.html.

15 United Nations Intergovernmental Panel on Climate Change, *Fourth Assessment Report*, p. 22.

16 Hansen et al., *Target Atmosphere CO_2*, p. 13.

RESOURCES

Books

Christianson, Gale E. *Greenhouse: The 200-Year Story of Global Warming.* New York: Walker and Company, 1999.

Gelbspan, Ross. *Boiling Point: How Politicians, Big Oil and Coal, Journalists, and Activists Are Fueling the Climate Crisis—and What We Can Do to Avert Disaster.* New York: Basic Books, 2004.

Gore, Al. *An Inconvenient Truth: The Planetary Emergency of Global Warming and What We Can Do About It.* Emmaus, Pa.: Rodale Press, 2006.

Horner, Christopher C. *The Politically Incorrect Guide to Global Warming and Environmentalism.* Washington, D.C.: Regnery Publishing, 2007.

Lomborg, Bjorn. *Cool It: The Skeptical Environmentalist's Guide to Global Warming.* New York: Alfred A. Knopf, 2007.

Lynas, Mark. *Six Degrees: Our Future on a Hotter Planet.* London: Fourth Estate, 2007.

Singer, S. Fred and Dennis T. Avery, *Unstoppable Global Warming: Every 1,500 Years.* Lanham, Md.: Rowman & Littlefield Publishers, 2007.

Reports

United Nations Intergovernmental Panel on Climate Change, *Fourth Assessment Report. Climate Change 2007: Synthesis Report. Summary for Policymakers.* Geneva, Switzerland, 2007.

Other Materials

"The Science of Climate Change," Senate Floor Statement by U.S. Senator James Inhofe, Chairman, Committee on the Environment and Public Works, July 28, 2003.

Statement of James Hansen to the Senate Committee on Energy and Natural Resources, June 23, 1988.

Web Sites
Governmental and International Organizations
The Intergovernmental Panel on Climate Change (IPCC)
http://www.ipcc.ch

A scientific intergovernmental body established by the World Meteorological Organization and the United Nations. Its role is to assess the latest scientific literature about human-caused climate change.

The United Nations Framework Convention on Climate Change (UNFCCC)

http://unfccc.int

This organization created a Conference of the Parties (COP), which is the treaty's standing legislative body. The COP meets periodically to consider measures aimed at reducing dangerous greenhouse gas emissions.

The U.S. Environmental Protection Agency (EPA)

http://www.epa.gov

This agency is in charge of enforcing federal environmental legislation.

Supporters of Climate Legislation

350.org

http://www.350.org

This newly formed coalition's goal is to persuade world leaders to take steps to bring the atmosphere's carbon dioxide concentration below 350 parts per million, which it considers the maximum safe level.

The Environmental Defense Fund

http://www.edf.org

The fund seeks innovative and cost-effective solutions to environmental problems.

The Natural Resources Defense Council

http://www.nrdc.org

The council describes its mission as safeguarding the Earth, its creatures, and the natural systems on which life depends.

The Pew Center for Climate Change

http://www.pewclimate.org

This organization brings together business leaders, policy makers, and scientists in an effort to identify measures that would protect the climate while sustaining economic growth.

The U.S. Climate Action Program (USCAP)

http://www.us-cap.org

An alliance of major corporations and nongovernmental organizations that favors developing "a regulated economy-wide, market-driven approach" to protecting the climate.

The World Resources Institute

http://www.wri.org

Its experts develop and promote policies aimed at protecting the Earth and improving people's lives.

Opponents of climate legislation

The American Enterprise Institute for Public Policy

http://www.aei.org

This institute supports individual liberty and responsibility and a strong foreign policy.

The Competitive Enterprise Institute

http://www.cei.org

It favors limited government and free enterprise solutions to economic and environmental problems.

The Copenhagen Consensus Center

http://www.copenhagenconsensus.com

A project headed by Bjorn Lomborg of the Copenhagen Business School. The center's goal is to identify the world's most serious problems and solve them in the most cost-efficient manner. The Center considers Kyoto-type measures a poor investment.

The George C. Marshall Institute

http://www.marshall.org

Its mission is to improve the use of science in making policy decisions.

The Heartland Institute

http://heartland.org

It favors free-market solutions to a variety of problems, including climate change. The institute has challenged Al Gore to a debate on global warming.

PICTURE CREDITS

PAGE

21: AFP/Getty Images
34: Newscom
39: Newscom

69: Newscom
73: Newscom

145

PAUL RUSCHMANN, J.D., is a legal analyst and writer based in Canton, Michigan. He received his undergraduate degree from the University of Notre Dame and his law degree from the University of Michigan. He is a member of the State Bar of Michigan. His areas of specialization include legislation, public safety, traffic and transportation, and trade regulation. He is also the author of 11 other books in the POINT/COUNTERPOINT series that deal with such issues as the military draft, indecency in the media, private property rights, and the war on terror. He can be found online at http://www.PaulRuschmann.com.

ALAN MARZILLI, M.A., J.D., lives in Birmingham, Alabama, and is a program associate with Advocates for Human Potential, Inc., a research and consulting firm based in Sudbury, Mass., and Albany, N.Y. He primarily works on developing training and educational materials for agencies of the federal government on topics such as housing, mental health policy, employment, and transportation. He has spoken on mental health issues in 30 states, the District of Columbia, and Puerto Rico; his work has included training mental health administrators, nonprofit management and staff, and people with mental illnesses and their families on a wide variety of topics, including effective advocacy, community-based mental health services, and housing. Marzilli has written several handbooks and training curricula that are used nationally and as far away as the U.S. territory of Guam. Additionally, he managed statewide and national mental health advocacy programs and worked for several public interest lobbying organizations while studying law at Georgetown University. Marzilli has written more than a dozen books, including numerous titles in the POINT/COUNTERPOINT series.